**PEARL
HARBOR
AND
HAWAII**

A MILITARY
HISTORY by th
Editors of the Army Time

PEARL HARBOR AND HAWAII

BONANZA BOOKS · NEW YORK

CONTENTS

FOREWORD

The United States, born in conflict, has survived only through an innate sense of self-defense.

Over the years, Americans have repeatedly been called upon to defend themselves and their commitments; from Bunker Hill on they have met challenges with varying degrees of enthusiasm and preparedness. The Revolution came very close to being lost. Washington was partly burned in the war of 1812. The United States was scarcely in a position to fight the Kaiser's Germany in 1917, even after the war was declared.

Following World War I, a revulsion against war and its seeming futility swept the country. Warships, tanks, artillery, trucks—the greater part of existing and effective military machinery—were scrapped. Stigma was associated with the uniform. The country limped into the 1930's naked to aggression. By 1938, the regular Army numbered only 183,477 officers and men.

When this shadow force marched off to maneuvers, the inventive spirit of old-line sergeants was sorely taxed. They fashioned cardboard cut-outs labelled "tank," substituted broom handles, barrels and stovepipes for AA-guns, mortars and field pieces. But the hard reality remained; the arsenal wouldn't fool even a third-rate enemy.

In September, 1939, the nation could not have repelled a determined invasion much more effectively than the Poles had when Nazi Germany overran their country. Nonetheless, President Roosevelt labelled America the "arsenal of democracy," and hoped thereby to reassure the beleaguered British.

Old Enfield rifles and French "75's," both relics of World War I, were examples of what little could be obtained from Army magazines. Lumbering bombers and obsolete pursuit planes flew in the air. Old battleships, traditionally the first line of naval seapower, were so slow they couldn't keep up with the few aircraft carriers then in commission.

The nation was in no condition to defeat an actual adversary, much less to scare off a potential one. Congress could not even make up its collective mind as to whether there should be a citizen army, mustered by conscription. However, a Selective Service Act was proclaimed in 1940 and renewed in August of 1941 by a margin of only one vote, 204-203, by the House of Representatives.

Then came December 7, and the Japanese attack upon our Pearl Harbor Naval Base. Isolation was suddenly ended. America's total resources were poured into a war effort that ultimately forged the mightiest fighting machine known in the history of man. Weaponry itself ranged from thumb-sized bombs (for the fighters behind the lines) to the nuclear weapons that could and did destroy whole cities.

Even while the Allies were winning an uphill fight on a global scale, their leaders were pondering the causes.

"For the second time in thirty years," declared Admiral Harry E. Yarnell, Commander of the Asiatic Fleet until 1939, "we have become involved in a gigantic war in spite of our policy of isolation. Evidently that policy doesn't work."

Lieutenant General Jonathan M. Wainwright, imprisoned by the Japanese after he was compelled to surrender Corregidor on May 6, 1942, and the highest-ranking American military man ever to be a P.O.W., would comment, "My men and I were victims of shortsightedness at home and of blind trust in the respectability of scheming aggressors. The price of our unpreparedness for a World War III would be death to millions of Americans and the disappearance from the earth of its greatest nation."

The unusual courage and sacrifice of young men had been called upon to rectify the "shortsightedness" of their elders. The lesson to be learned was the old Boy Scout motto: "Be prepared."

The philosopher, George Hegel, spoke the truth 150 years ago when he observed, "What history and experience teach is this: that people and governments never have learned anything from history."

This book is the story of Pearl Harbor. And indirectly of Hawaii itself. The attack and the subsequent war years, when patriotism attained new pinnacles, should not and must not be forgotten if, in contradiction to Hegel, we can ever cease to repeat the mistakes of the past.

CHAPTER 1

The volcanic Hawaiian chain or "ridge" lies 2200 miles west of California. It extends from its principal group of eight islands to little Midway, 1600 miles to the northwest. All the islands are, in effect, mountain tops, rising above an immense continent under the Pacific Ocean.

History and legend agree that the first Hawaiians arrived on the islands with their women and children in about the fifth century A.D. They also brought with them pigs, dogs, which were used for food, and chickens. These first settlers were seafarers who had probably started out from southern Asia, discovering and populating all the inhabited islands of the Pacific.

In all likelihood the Spanish first set foot in Polynesia in the sixteenth century. However, the English took credit for the discovery in January, 1778. Captain James Cook, at fifty years of age a seasoned explorer of the Pacific Ocean, was en route to the Polar Sea when interest in an unexpected landfall led him ashore on Kauai. Since he spoke Tahitian, he could make himself understood. He learned, among other things, that Kauai was but one of an island group, the other major islands being Hawaii, Maui and Oahu.

Before he departed, Cook named these bright, balmy outcroppings in the Pacific in honor of the Earl of Sandwich, First Lord of the Admiralty. They became the "Sandwich Islands" and were so labelled by the world's cartographers for several decades.

Captain Cook returned to the Islands ten months later, but this time he overstayed his welcome. During a fight that broke out between the islanders and the English seamen, the Captain was killed.

Some six years passed after Cook's violent end before another foreign ship dropped anchor at the Islands. By then fur trade between Alaska and China was thriving and Hawaii became a natural stopover.

In 1787, the Austrian East India Company sent out the *Imperial Eagle,* which dropped anchor at Hawaii en route to Canton. In 1789, the first American vessel arrived in Hawaii, the *Columbia Rediviva,* 220 tons, full-rigged, with two decks, and armed with ten guns; she was commanded by Captain Robert Gray, the discoverer of the Columbia River.

Next from the States was the *Hancock,* a brig which came in 1791, followed by many more trading ships flying Old Glory. Since Europe had become enmeshed in a war with Napoleon, the fur trade was almost entirely left to the Americans.

American missionaries set sail in October, 1819, from Boston to "save" the heathen Hawaiians. Their efforts met with success. Soon, Hawaiians observed Sunday in the Puritan manner. There was no uncalled-for work or play, only religious worship.

The missionaries' influence eliminated much of the absolute power of the kings and chiefs and culminated in 1840 with Kamehameha III's Declaration of Rights and a Constitution. With this document, inequities would go and the people would have a greater political voice. Wages, as low as $4 a month for coolies in the sugar fields, started to move, if very slowly, upward.

With the advent of steam sloops, the Islands were but a week's journey from California. Their relationship to the economy and security of the United States was already apparent. Matthew Fontaine Maury, the hydrographer and navigator, was among those who foresaw Hawaii's military significance.

Commodore Charles Wilkes touched at Hawaii in 1840 during a government exploring expedition in the Pacific. After rounding the channel entrance between Keahi Point and Holokahili Point to what would be known as Pearl Harbor ("Wai Momi," the Polynesian River of Pearls), Wilkes concluded, "If the water upon the bar should be deepened, which I doubt not can be effected, it would afford the best and most capacious harbor in the Pacific." Earlier Royal Navy soundings had inspired much the same reaction. The entrance, only 375 yards wide, and much of that mudflats at low tide, presented a still greater challenge. Once over this bar, however, Wilkes found the anchorage to be completely landlocked, with volcanic ridges sheltering the harbor from the north and east. Typhoons were no threat, as they did not move so far east.

The year after Wilkes left, in February, 1843, the independence of Hawaii was briefly threatened when Lord George Paulet tried to force secession to Great Britain. He went so far as to raise the Union Jack and suggest that British subjects take refuge on the Royal Navy's men-of-war should the local inhabitants "resent" his tactics.

The presence at the same time of the USS *Constitution* under

Captain Lawrence Kearney, commanding the Navy's East India Squadron, had something to do with protecting the neutrality of the Islands and guaranteeing the continuance of the Hawaiian flag.

"That little squadron," the Secretary of the Navy's report for the year would note in praise, "has done all that could have been expected of it and it deserves much credit for its great vigilance and activity and for the prudence and sound discretion with which Captain Kearney has acquitted himself." The other member of "that little squadron" was the sloop-of-war *Boston*.

As a second "hands off" step, President Tyler extended the Monroe Doctrine to encompass Hawaii and the easternmost reaches of the Pacific.

During the Civil War, Great Britain ordered warships to Honolulu frequently, noting that control of the entire North Pacific would pass to the nation that based strong fleet units there. Yet the United States' main use of the Islands had been as a coaling station. Ranking admirals had discounted their potential as a base for operations against the Confederate commerce raiders; they were soon proved wrong. Even after the surrender at Appomattox in April, 1865, the Confederate *Shenandoah* had captured or destroyed seventy vessels of the New Bedford whaling fleet in the Bering Sea between Alaska and Russia.

After the wasting War of the Rebellion, the United States was able to look beyond its immediate shores once more. Its relationship with the Hawaiian Islands grew still warmer with the succession of King David Kalakaua.

The following year, Major General John McAllister Schofield, General Sherman's 23rd Corps commander in the Atlanta campaign, arrived with a survey party. On the basis of his soundings, he reported to the Secretary of War that "the harbor of Ewa or Pearl River is a fine sheet of deep water extending inland about six miles from its mouth."

He observed, however, that the entrance was blocked by a coral reef two to three fathoms (twelve to eighteen feet) in depth. The dredged channel, Schofield affirmed, would provide access to a harbor "spacious enough for a large number of vessels to ride at anchor in perfect security against all storms."

Congress was inspired to debate the value of Pearl Harbor over Midway Island, already claimed for the United States following a visit in 1867 by the steam frigate, USS *Lackawanna*. Admiral Alfred Mahan proved a strong proponent of the Hawaiian anchorage, noting, "The distance from Hawaii to San Francisco is approximately the same as that to the Marquesas, Tahiti, Samoa, the Gilbert and Marshall Islands, and a compass laid out to this distance would draw a

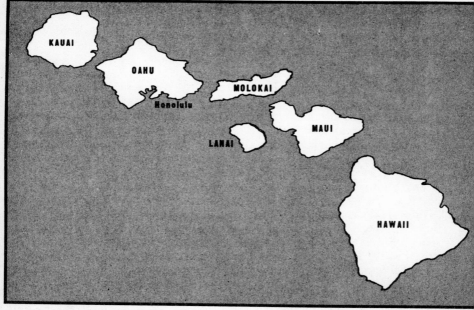

The islands of Hawaii.

JACK AUDRIDGE

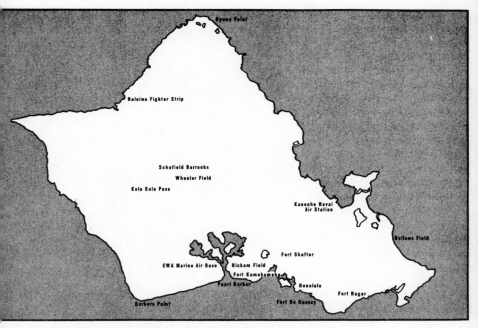

Military and naval installations on Oahu in 1941.

JACK AUDRIDGE

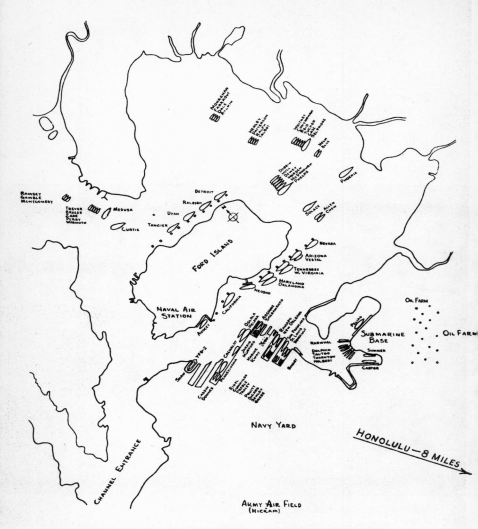

The position of ships in Pearl Harbor just before the attack.

Secretary of War Stimson.

Ford Island, in the center of Pearl Harbor, looked like this in the fall of 1941. Hickam Field is to the left, top of photograph.

circle around Hawaii with its circumference touching all those distant neighbors of Hawaii."

The 1870's proved to be years of modest prosperity. While the population did not exceed 50,000, it was steadily increasing. The Treaty of Reciprocity, which was signed in Washington in 1876, was certain to spur sugar production, then about 12,000 tons a year. The potential was and had been much higher.

Kalakaua, meanwhile, was seeking too many royal prerogatives. His subjects forced him to sign a new constitution that fettered his too-free will. It had come none too soon; he was in the process of suggesting a marriage alliance between his family and that of the Emperor of Japan, which would have presaged no good either for Hawaii or the United States.

Since the revised constitution had reined the "merry monarch's" freewheeling proclivities, he was induced to grant America the "exclusive right to enter the harbor of Pearl River . . . and to establish . . . a coaling and repair station for the use of vessels of the United States."

The same treaty also allowed the start of blasting operations through the coral bar obstructing Pearl Harbor. The reef and surrounding rocks were so hard as to be called "lava glass." It would be more than a decade before engineers were ready for the challenge.

Kalakaua died in 1891 during a visit to San Francisco. Liliuokalani, his corpulent sister, succeeded him, only to be deposed after a bloodless coup.

Sanford Ballard Dole, a lawyer and missionary's son, was then chosen to lead a provisional government. Dole lost no time in requesting annexation by the United States. President Grover Cleveland, more concerned with domestic matters, wasn't interested. In 1894, Hawaii was proclaimed a republic, with Dole the first president.

The outbreak of the war with Spain in 1898 again accented the strategic importance of Hawaii in the Pacific. Washington belatedly recognized Cleveland's shortsightedness as Congress by joint resolution annexed the Hawaiian Islands—as of August 12, 1898, the day the war ended by protocol.

Soon, Honolulu echoed to the tramp of military boots as troops sailed westward to garrison the Philippines, next to suppress the insurrection. Soldiers rode the streetcars free and were provided coffee and doughnuts at Red Cross canteens.

The old Navy station at Honolulu had become the Naval Coal Depot, with storage capacity increased from 1000 to 20,000 tons; it was redesignated the "U.S. Naval Station." The land for its expansion cost $52,000, or less than half the value of one acre in the area today.

The Navy needed its base, and fast. Dredging commenced for a two hundred-foot wide, thirty-foot deep channel, which would be two-thirds of a mile long. The $3.5 million contract was awarded the Hawaiian Dredging Company, headed by Walter Dillingham.

In January, 1905, the 829-ton gunboat USS *Petrel,* whistle blowing, banners flying from twin masts, chugged into Pearl Harbor with eighteen feet of water still below her keel. She ushered in a new era for the United States and the Navy.

The Army by now was well dug in. Camp McKinley had been established at the base of the spectacular Diamond Head promontory, after the termination of hostilities with Spain. The permanent garrison, even so, was something less than formidable: one battalion, the third of the Second Volunteer Engineers.

The growth potential of military reservations was considerably more auspicious than the number of those billeted in the Islands. Nineteen miles northwest of Honolulu, a 14,400-acre tract was set aside as the future home of Schofield Barracks, recalling the general who had surveyed Oahu for such purposes more than a quarter of a century earlier.

Since it would take some time to put in reservoirs for the large post, a much smaller one, Fort Shafter, named after General William Shafter, who commanded Army troops in Cuba, was commissioned on the western extremities of Honolulu.

Fort Ruger came along in 1906, embracing 755 acres, about half the size of Shafter.

Two years later, the House Committee on Naval Affairs, continuing to be worried about the nation's Pacific flanks, asserted, "An enemy in possession of Hawaii could harass and threaten our entire western coast. With our own fleet operating from a well-equipped base at Pearl Harbor, no fleet from the Orient would find it practicable to threaten our coast."

In July of the same year, 1908, the Great White Fleet, dispatched on a world cruise by President Theodore Roosevelt, called at Hawaii. But the reception was entirely disappointing. As far as the islanders were concerned, it was a bit too soon after America's military operations in that ocean. Officers from the sixteen battleships and escorts reported a generally sullen reception. The Polynesians kept away, not exactly unimpressed, but in likelihood a bit frightened at so much flaunting of power.

The "heavies" were followed later by the 13,680-ton armored cruiser *California,* the first ship of the battle line to enter Pearl Harbor itself.

Governor Walter Frear was on hand the next year, 1909, at Schofield Barracks' first review. Brigadier General John J. Pershing, newly married and en route to the Philippines, was also present.

Service life in the Islands appeared on an upswing. The Honolulu *Advertiser,* which was founded in 1856, mused, "Who knows? It may be that there will be 20,000 soldiers stationed at the local forts at some future time."

With the naval base in active and increasing operation, a dry dock was needed. In September, 1909, work was started on one to be 589 feet long. And for the next four years, while the clouds of international tension and uncertainty darkened, defense activities in Hawaii pretty much centered about the construction of the wonderful new dry dock. On the Army side, the garrison, far from the paper's dreamy 20,000, wiled away the hot hours in drills, bivouacs and target practice, mostly with side arms and rifles. Field pieces in any quantity or heavy coastal batteries were yet to come.

Then, in February, 1913, from the direction of Pearl Harbor came sounds not unlike the volcanoes over on the "Big Island," Hawaii. The still incomplete dock had sunk "upwards." The bottom, with too much pressure on the sides, had heaved skyward along with huge pilings, hurtling up just like projectiles. Derricks, a steam donkey engine, concrete mixers and winches tumbled down into the shattered pit in a massive heap of rubble and twisted cables. Millions of board feet of lumber were reduced to giant splinters.

It was, Secretary of the Navy Josephus Daniels postscripted, "the naval disaster of the year." Not until 1919 would the rebuilt and redesigned dock, now a fifth of a mile long, be ready "for occupancy."

CHAPTER 2

With America's entry into the 1914-18 war slogans vied with flags to enliven Honolulu's sidewalks: "Grow Your Own Food," or "Eat More Bananas!" in addition to the continuing Liberty Loan pleas. In a few months, the Islands had raised $3 million for war bonds.

In August, 1914, 1084 residents of the Islands were called up in the draft. Ten thousand National Guardsmen replaced the regular Army troops who went to the mainland, and in some cases to France.

In February, 1918, Washington was worried that newly Bolshevized Russia would by some "intrigue and treachery" aid Germany and divide Alaska and Hawaii between themselves. First, however, the two powers would have to seize these American territories. It did not seem so likely.

Early in the war an Army flying center was established at Fort Kamehameha. This was located at the entrance to Pearl Harbor, which had become the "backbone of naval power in the Pacific," according to Secretary Daniels.

Captains John F. Curry and John D. Brooks, of the Aeronautical Division of the Signal Corps, brought the 6th Aero Squadron to Hawaii: twelve enlisted men, three airplanes strong. The Sixth was headquartered on Ford Island, in Pearl Harbor.

Then, with the Armistice, November 11, 1918, the World War ended and the flurry and excitement, band music and parades suddenly were gone from Hawaii. Peacetime had returned.

Naval aviation was expanded when both the secretaries of war and of the Navy agreed to a joint use of Ford Island. On December 19, the USS *Chicago* dropped anchor, bearing with her four seaplanes together with forty-nine officers and men under Lieutenant Commander R. D. Kirkpatrick to form the "Pacific Air Detachment."

A temporary submarine base was moved to its present location on

Admiral of the Fleet Isoroku Yamamoto was the architect of the Pearl Harbor attack.

Secretary of the Navy Frank Knox.

Admiral Husband E. Kimmel.

A few days before Pearl Harbor, Special Envoy Kurusu (r) presented his credentials to Secretary of State Hull (c). Ambassador Nomura is on the left.

WORLD WIDE PHOTO

Lieutenant General Walter Short.

The commander of this Japanese midget submarine, Ensign Kazuo Saka-maki, made shore off Bellows Field although his shipmate was drowned.

the Naval Base. Although primarily west coast-based, the Pacific Fleet now numbered two hundred units.

The postwar years brought Hawaii its second air base, Wheeler Field, established adjacent to Schofield Barracks on Oahu. Named for Major Sheldon H. Wheeler, commander of Luke Field until he was killed in an air crash on July 12, 1921, the base was dedicated on Armistice Day, November 11, 1922.

The next year, Commander John Rodgers, descendant of a distinguished naval family, commissioned the Naval Air Station at Ford Island. In September, 1925, Rodgers, with a crew of four, took off in the lead of two seaplanes, bound from San Francisco Bay to Hawaii. One aircraft was forced down by engine trouble, but Rodgers kept going.

Short of his goal and having missed a station ship for refueling, Rodgers himself landed in the ocean. For ten days, as the world gave him up for lost, he maneuvered his twin-engine craft like a boat, using wing fabric for sails, until he sighted Kauai. A submarine gave his plane a tow for the last twenty miles to enable him to complete the first "flight" from the west coast to the Islands.

Altogether 1925 was a great naval year. A fleet review brought 137 ships to Hawaii, lined up at one time all the way from Waikiki into Pearl. Receptions, dances, all manner of entertainment greeted the crews.

On a Sunday morning in February, 1932, an air-minded admiral, Harry Yarnell, commanding the Carrier Battle Force, dispatched 152 aircraft from the sister carriers, *Lexington* and *Saratoga*, in a surprise "raid" on Pearl Harbor. Theoretically, his squadrons obliterated all airplanes on the ground and sank most of the ships at anchor.

Japanese naval attachés in Honolulu read about the exercise and were so impressed that they filed copious dispatches to Tokyo. The meaning seemed to escape American military leaders, especially the so-called battleship admirals who couldn't believe the losses would have occurred "for real."

About the same time, the Air Corps did much the same—flying through the Kole-Kole pass in the four thousand-foot Waianae Mountains, just behind Schofield, to pounce on bases and outposts on the western half of the island.

One of the nation's largest air bases thus far constructed was dedicated in 1935: Hickam Field, hacked at a cost of $15 million out of 2500 acres of sugar cane and tangled keawe. The work in itself brought considerable relief to Oahu from the depression years.

The field was named in memory of Lieutenant Colonel Horace M. Hickam, killed in an accident in Texas in 1934.

Situated as they were, the Hawaiian Islands proved a natural fuel and rest stop for all planes as well as their pioneer pilots. In 1935, Amelia Earhart flew solo from Honolulu to California in eighteen hours, sixteen minutes, or about four hours slower than Clipper time.

And all the while Hawaii's stature as the west coast's outer defenses grew, spurred by the concerns of the day. Japan, in a "banzai" mood, was carving out her "coprosperity" sphere in Asia. Having already annexed Korea in 1910, Japan had more lately marched into Manchuria and was bogged down in China, striving to slog her way farther into the interior.

But islands, such as the Marianas, the Marshalls and Carolines, mandated to the Empire of the Rising Sun for her part in World War I, were more of a threat to American interests than Tokyo's mainland encroachments. Directly menaced were the Philippines, Samoa, Guam, Wake, Midway and the Hawaiian group.

As time passed, relations between the United States and Japan deteriorated, with scant hope of improvement. The gunboat USS *Panay* was bombed and sunk by Japanese planes in the Yangtze River on December 12, 1937, with the loss of two lives. Apologies were followed by indemnities, but there remained little doubt in the Department of State that the aggressive act had been no accident.

Millions of dollars for defense were appropriated by Congress in an endeavor to prepare the Islands for war. Defense workers arrived in ever greater numbers and additional troops, supplies and equipment were shipped in. The Hawaiian Air Force of the Army was activated. Army troops, which had fluctuated between thirteen thousand and fifteen thousand in the decade before 1935, now numbered twenty-five thousand. The Navy based five thousand officers and men ashore and many thousands more on ships in these waters.

In 1940 the Islands were visited by General George Catlett Marshall, the first Army Chief of Staff to do so. Returning, General Marshall signed an aide memoir: "The island of Oahu, due to its fortifications, its garrison and its physical characteristics, is believed to be the strongest fortress in the world."

Later, he would amplify in testimony, ". . . we had no intimation that that command [the Hawaiian Department] was not ready and I think we had every reason to believe that it was ready."

Conceivably the Chief of Staff was not as *au courant* with the threat from Tokyo as other senior officials. For example, Rear Admiral Joseph K. Taussig, destroyer squadron hero of World War I, told a Senate Naval Affairs Committee in April, 1940, that war with Japan was "inevitable," since the Imperial warlords' long-range plan was that of world conquest "after first crushing the United States."

President Roosevelt seemed to believe so himself, for he convinced Congress to authorize funds for a "two-ocean" Navy. In May of the same year he ordered the Pacific Fleet to move out of San Pedro and defend the hemisphere from Honolulu. Its commanding officer, Admiral James O. Richardson, was not at all pleased. "It's a mouse-trap," he fumed, thereby incurring the wrath of the chief executive. Richardson felt that the fleet was a big, fat, sitting duck, and he was not far from the truth.

Developments accelerated. In September, Tokyo entered the Tri-Partite Pact with Germany and Italy, which now became popularly known as the Rome-Berlin-Tokyo Axis, aimed blatantly at the United States and all of the democracies.

On New Year's Day, 1941, Ambassador Joseph E. Grew, in his Tokyo embassy, confided in his diary, "There's a lot of talk that the Japanese in case of a break with the United States are planning to go all out in a surprise attack on Pearl Harbor."

President Roosevelt, who had let it be known that he considered the Imperial Japanese as the "Prussians of the East," decided in July, 1941, that he was sick of "babying along" these militarists on the other side of the Pacific Ocean. In concert with England, he ordered Cordell Hull, the Secretary of State, to freeze all Japanese assets.

Suddenly, the warlords of Nippon were denied oil, iron ore, manganese, scrap and many raw materials voraciously craved by their machines of aggression.

In early September, Premier Prince Fumimaro Konoye wrote in his diary, following a meeting of the cabinet:

In view of the present pressing situation, the offensives of the United States, Britain, the Netherlands, etc., toward Japan and the flexibility of the national power of the Empire, the enforcement of measures regarding the southern regions shall be made as follows:

1. The Empire shall complete war preparations with the last decade of October as the aim under the determination not to mind war with the United States (Britain and the Netherlands) for the purpose of guaranteeing its self-existence and self-defense.

2. In parallel to it, the Empire shall have recourse to diplomatic means in dealing with the United States and Britain and endeavor to have its demands attained.

3. In case there is found no way still for attainment of our demands even in the first decade of October, the Empire shall at once determine upon war with the United States (Britain and the Netherlands) . . . [1]

There wasn't much air power on Hawaii to offset "war

Herbert Feis, *The Road to Pearl Harbor;* see Bibliography.

preparations"—227 planes at Hickam, Wheeler and Bellows Fields, one-half of which were classed obsolescent. There were only six operational 4-engined B-17 bombers.

Konoye, a "moderate," did not last much longer. His cabinet fell the next month, and he was replaced by Lieutenant General Hideki Tojo, a tough, single-minded militarist called "kamisori," or "razor blade." He had already asserted with incredible naïveté that "Japan must be able to fight China and Russia at *the same time.*"

However, seemingly as an avowal of reconciliation between Japan and the United States, Tojo rushed a second envoy, Saburo Kurusu, to Washington in great haste. He was to supplement the "peace talks" of the regular ambassador, Kichisaburo Nomura, a retired naval officer.

Curiously enough, on the day before Saburo called at the old State, War and Navy Department in Washington to present his credentials, Ensign Kazuo Sakamaki and several other members of the Japanese Navy's "Special Attack Forces" assembled at the Kure Naval Base. Sakamaki, who was twenty-three and the commander of a two-man midget submarine, listened to a reading: "These are the orders from the headquarters of the General Staff of the Imperial Navy. You are herewith to take positions of readiness for war with the United States of America."

CHAPTER 3

By late November, 1941, Japanese-American talks had trailed off into icy bickering, then ceased altogether.

Secretary Hull was so worried that he urged his "boss" to come home without delay from Warm Springs, Georgia. The President had been spending a long Thanksgiving weekend there with fellow polio victims.

Roosevelt was back in Washington Monday noon, December 1. A new crop of "magic" code messages lay on his desk. These comprised Tokyo's diplomatic radio correspondence with her embassy in Washington and had been decoded by the Navy's and Army's "purple" machine. The implied threats to the Pacific had grown to such an extent that Admiral Harold R. Stark, Chief of Naval Operations, saw fit to send a warning to Admiral Husband E. Kimmel, commanding the United States Pacific Fleet. The successor to the outspoken Admiral Richardson was a 1904 graduate of the Naval Academy, but one year behind the Chief of Naval Operations.

"This dispatch," the message read, "is to be considered a war warning. Negotiations with Japan looking toward stabilization of conditions in the Pacific have ceased and an aggressive move by Japan is expected within the next few days. The number and equipment of Japanese troops and the organization of naval task forces indicates an amphibious expedition against either the Philippines, Thai or Kra Peninsula[2] or possibly Borneo. Execute an appropriate defensive deployment preparatory to carrying out the tasks assigned in WPL46. Inform district and Army authorities. A similar warning is being sent by War Department . . ."

Stark then wrote "Hubby" Kimmel a personal note: ". . . neither (Roosevelt nor Hull) would be surprised over a Japanese surprise attack. From many angles an attack on the Philippines would be the

[2] The Isthmus of Kra, the northern waist of present Malaysia, on the Gulf of Siam.

most embarrassing thing that could happen to us. . . . I do not give it the weight others do. . . . I have generally held that it was not time for the Japanese to proceed against Russia. I still do. Also, I still rather look for an advance into Thailand, Indo-China, Burma Road areas as the most likely.

"I won't go into the pros and cons of what the United States may do. I will be damned if I know. I wish I did. The only thing I do know is that we may do most anything and that's the only thing I know to be prepared for; or we may do nothing—I think it is more likely to be 'anything.' "

For all its good and friendly intent, Stark's letter only augmented the mounting atmosphere of confusion which was all but suffocating the Pacific military leaders. General Marshall had, at the same time, moved along his own alert to Lieutenant General Walter Short, commanding the Hawaiian Department, which then comprised slightly more than forty thousand men and approximately twenty-five hundred officers:

"Negotiations with Japan appear to be terminated to all practical purposes with only the barest possibilities that the Japanese government might come back and offer to continue. Japanese future action unpredictable but hostile action possible at any moment. If hostilities cannot—repeat not—be avoided the United States desires that Japan commit the first overt act. This policy should not—repeat not—be construed as restricting you to a course of action that might jeopardize your defense. Prior to hostile Japanese action you are directed to undertake such reconnaissance and other measures as you deem necessary but these measures should be carried out so as not—repeat not—to alarm civil population or disclose intent . . . undertake no offensive action until Japan has committed an overt act."

The general in Honolulu responded: "Department alerted to prevent sabotage. Liaison with Navy."

The sabotage alert was the lowest of various states of preparedness. Scarcely noticeable to Hawaiians, either in dispositions of soldiers or guns, this alert was in some of its provisions ridiculously self-defeating. For example, planes were to be grouped on the fields so that one or two sentries could effectively guard them. They also made an enviable target.

Live ammunition, especially for the large caliber guns, was supposed to be locked up so that none had access without obtaining the key or keys from the duty officer. In some cases, the duty officer then had to locate, if he could, the ordnance watch officer.

To swing the huge coastal guns at Fort de Russey, at Waikiki Beach, or Fort "Kam" guarding the Pearl Harbor channel into full "ready" might require hours, from chasing down the precious keys to finding men to trundle up the shells and projectiles as well as to man the complicated batteries themselves.

On many of the ships at the Naval Base, ammunition also was tightly padlocked, some of the gun sights removed, and electrical circuits to fire control directors defused. A number of torpedoes had been dismantled in the search for a rumored new marine growth!

As the final days of peace ticked irrevocably away, messages of an increasingly suspicious nature whispered through the "purple" decoding machine in Washington. Already, the desks of the Army's G-2 and the Office of Naval Intelligence were relatively heavy with such intercepted dispatches, especially between the Japanese Consul Nagao Kita, at Honolulu, and the Tokyo Foreign Office. Japan's leaders apparently were unaware for the full duration of the war of the extent of United States' counter-intelligence and ability to unravel their top secret codes.

Kita had been describing in detail the fleet anchorage positions, the entrance and exit to Pearl of capital warships and, through a dentist confederate, Dr. Motokazu Mori, other matters of normally classified nature which should not have been so intriguing to foreign nationals.

There were, at the same time, two real puzzlers to American intelligence officers:

1. A message spelling out "east wind rain," which was the code phrase for endangered Japan—U.S. relations.

2. The total disappearance of the 10 Japanese aircraft carriers radio transmission. This formidable force had in effect vanished from American monitors in the last days of November.

On December 3, a telling message was received: "Urgent instructions were sent yesterday to Japanese diplomats and consular posts at Hong Kong, Singapore, Batavia, Manila, Washington and London to destroy most of their codes and ciphers at once and to burn all other important and confidential secret documents."

After a five-minute interval, another dispatch: "Ordered London, Hong Kong, Singapore and Manila to destroy machine. Batavia machine already sent to Tokyo. December 2, Washington directed to destroy all but one copy of other systems and all secret documents. British Admiralty London today reports Embassy London has complied."

On Thursday, December 4, the large aircraft carrier, *Lexington*, led Task Force 2 out of her Ford Island anchorage. Aboard were twenty-five Marine planes and their pilots destined for Midway Island. Another carrier, the *Enterprise*, was already en route to Wake with a consignment of Navy planes.

Thus, there were no carriers in Pearl Harbor by the end of the first week in December. The other "heavies," the battleships of the Pacific Fleet, stayed in port since they were some ten knots too slow to keep up with the swift carriers. With three exceptions, the battleships were moored meticulously, side by side, close to the shores of Ford Island, which also served as a naval air station. The flagship of Admiral Kimmel, the *Pennsylvania*, sat in drydock. The *Nevada* and the *California* were moored separately, but adjacent to the others.

All of this was relayed to Tokyo by the efficient Kita, as he summed up, "The *Lexington* and five heavy cruisers left port . . . the following ships were in port on the afternoon of the 5th; 8 battleships, 3 light cruisers, 16 destroyers."

In Washington, meanwhile, a curious mixture of concern, apathy and naïve optimism was evident. As an example of the latter or, perhaps more aptly, delusion, the affable Secretary of the Navy, Frank Knox, was writing his annual State-of-the-Navy message, for release Sunday morning: "I am proud to report that the American people may feel fully confident in the Navy. In my opinion . . . the United States Navy is second to none."

And on an inspection tour in Puerto Rico, Ralph Owen Brewster, the Republican Senator from Maine, was quoted as stating without qualification, "The United States Navy can defeat the Japanese Navy any place and at any time."

At the White House, the President was reading a confidential dossier on the latest Japanese potential for aggression. The stock-taking included the sighting of a formidable taskforce of seventy ships apparently headed towards Malaya.

For a moment, the chief executive looked up at his Naval aide, Captain John R. Beardall, to ask, somewhat enigmatically: "When do you think *it* will happen?"

"Most any time," Beardall replied in the same vein.

As the week drew to a close, Saturday, December 6, "any time" began to seem—to a few intelligence officers in Washington—much sooner than later. Early that morning, a new dispatch from the Tokyo Foreign Office to Ambassador Nomura in Washington was decoded by the Navy and Army: "This separate message is a very long one. I will send it in 14 parts and I imagine you will receive it tomorrow. . . . I want you to please keep it secret for the time being. . . ."

From other sources, G-2 learned that the Japanese embassy was starting to burn its codebooks, and so informed Army intelligence at Fort Shafter, Honolulu.

At 10:40 A.M., the same Saturday, the Department of State was advised by its London embassy: "British Admiralty reports that at 3 A.M. London time this morning two parties seen off Cambodia Point,

An Aichi 99, VAL dive bomber moves in for the attack.

Smoke rises from the border of Hickam Field. In the fore-ground (l to r) are the battleships Nevada and Arizona (not yet hit) with the supply ship Vestal moored outboard, the Tennessee with apparently a geyser of water on her port side, the West Virginia, the Maryland, the Oklahoma and the tanker Neosho, which was about to make a dramatic dash for safety. This photograph was included in captured Japanese documents.

A second photograph captured from the
Japanese showing the first bombs falling.

sailing slowly westward Kra, 14 hours distant in time. First party 25 transports, 6 cruisers, 10 destroyers. Second party, 10 transports, 2 cruisers. 10 destroyers. . . . ''

Both Secretary Hull and Secretary of War Henry L. Stimson agreed that "we and our friends" were "in imminent danger." Stimson altered his weekend social engagements so as to be as close to the telephone as possible. Hull was too unwell these days even to plan any such activities.

At the White House, pawing over a sheaf of the latest intelligence reports handed to him from several sources, Roosevelt remarked to a caller, Budget Director Harold Smith, "We might be at war with Japan. . . ." To Smith, it sounded like nothing more than an off-hand remark.

After lunch, the chief executive held a twenty-minute meeting with the British ambassador, Lord Halifax, then commenced dictating a personal appeal to Emperor Hirohito: ". . . during the past few weeks it has become clear to the world that Japanese military, naval and air forces have been sent to southern Indo-China in such large numbers as to create a reasonable doubt on the part of other nations that this continuing concentration . . . is not defensive in its character. . . . It is clear that a continuance of such a situation is unthinkable. . . ."

When he finished, he ordered it relayed through his ambassador, Joseph Grew in Tokyo. The note did reach the Tokyo cable office in relatively short order, but there it would be delayed for more than ten hours, too late for Grew to make use of it.

For most people, this was just a routine, but unusually mild Saturday afternoon in Washington. Before December's long shadows fell, even the War, Navy and State Departments were virtually empty of their staffs. Only communications, intelligence and various duty watch offices remained open. But some of those with lights on were busier than anyone had ever known.

Colonel Rufus Bratton, chief of Army Intelligence's Far East Section, was one such. Another was somewhat his counterpart in the sister section of the Office of Naval Intelligence, Lieutenant Commander Alwin D. Kramer.

The pair had been wrestling with the translation of the announced fourteen-part message from Tokyo all afternoon. By early evening all but the last part had been completed. Wordy, assertive, purposely vague, the rambling message, intended for ultimate delivery by the Japanese ambassador to the State Department, did not—in those thirteen sections—announce a break in diplomatic relations.

It did say "the Japanese Government cannot tolerate the perpetuation" of Anglo-American "collusion" in the East. The two officers, who were familiar with Oriental reasoning, were extremely concerned. They had to let higher-ups know about those parts thus-far decoded. The frustrating aspect was that not many of these officials seemed to be home that evening.

Brigadier General Sherman Miles, in charge of G-2, had left his Georgetown residence for a dinner party. In the "T.O." (table of organization) it was Miles' duty and prerogative to inform the Chief of Staff, General Marshall, of any and all military matters.

Admiral Stark was at the theater. Rear Admiral Richmond Kelly Turner, the powerful Chief of War Plans, did not pick up his telephone.

However, Kramer delivered a copy of the thirteen parts to Lieutenant Lester Schulz, standing the Navy's confidential mail watch at the White House—and Roosevelt *was* in. He received the young officer in the Oval Room, where he had been talking with his adviser and long-time erony, Harry Hopkins.

It seemed to Schulz, waiting somewhat uncomfortably in silence, that the President spent "perhaps ten minutes" poring over the thirteen parts. Hopkins himself paced restlessly back and forth like a caged creature. Finally, Roosevelt turned to Hopkins and observed in rather resigned tones: "This means war."

Before the young naval officer was dismissed, Harry Hopkins commented ruefully that it was "too bad" the United States "could not strike the first blow."

Roosevelt replied while, curiously, nodding his head as if in agreement, "No, you can't do that. We are a democracy and a peaceful people."

As Schulz was leaving he heard the chief executive say he would try to reach "Betty." This was the singular nickname for Admiral Stark.

Kramer, meanwhile, had continued his calls. He found Frank Knox at his apartment in the Wardman Park Hotel. The Secretary of the Navy read the thirteen parts, then telephoned Secretary Stimson to arrange for a ten o'clock morning meeting.

The lieutenant commander next drove to the Virginia home of Rear Admiral Theodore Stark Wilkinson, Chief of Naval Intelligence. It so happened that General Miles and Captain Beardall were dining with the admiral.

The somewhat oblique note sounded to Wilkinson like "a diplomatic paper." Sherman Miles attributed "little military significance" to it.

The party was breaking up. When Sherman Miles reached his own home he found a message waiting to phone Colonel Bratton. He did so, then informed his Far East expert that he saw no reason for "waking up" General Marshall.

At 11:30, Admiral Stark came back to his official quarters from the theater and returned President Roosevelt's call. A friend with him obtained the impression that the Chief of Naval Operations was "five or ten minutes" in a second floor room with a direct line to the White House.

The gist of the conversation between these two influential figures was not, nor is now, a matter of record.

About midnight a weary, increasingly worried Kramer finished his rounds at the suburban Maryland residence of Admiral Turner. The latter explained he had been in and out walking his Lhasa terriers, which he raised.

Turner put on his eyeglasses, carefully read the long communication, then asserted it was not his "function" to "take any action."

Sunday morning, December 7, 1941, was already a few minutes old. And most of the nation's capital, those whose opinion could sway the destinies of millions of other people, were well tucked into their beds and, presumably, sleeping quite soundly.

CHAPTER | **4**

Saturday afternoon in Honolulu faded into "a clear, tropical night." Such was the opinion of Takeo Yoshikawa, one of the abnormally large number of 217 assistant consuls working for Japanese Consul Kita.

Yoshikawa, however, was a rather special subordinate, who had assembled since his arrival in April a great deal of week-to-week intelligence on the United States' armed forces. He had carried his sense of mission so far as to swim underwater in vital areas to search out submarine nets.

In the evenings, he could spy in grand style from the Shuncho-ro Restaurant in the vicinity of Aiea Heights. While through binoculars he watched harbor activity, he partook of native dishes and wine, always with sufficient female company.

Takeo had a wide choice of dining companions; with 160,000 persons of Japanese descent dwelling in the Islands in 1941 out of a total population of not quite 424,000. On the other hand, all of Consul Kita's paid entourage were nationals of his own country. He feared, with reason, to "trust" Hawaiian-Japanese.

However, on this "clear, tropical" evening, Yoshikawa was in the consulate on Nuuanu Avenue, "deserted except for myself . . . and a bored code clerk." He had just dispatched his last message: ". . . no indication of air or sea alert wired to nearby islands."

In an especially relaxed mood, as he would recall, he reflected on the importance Vice Admiral Chuichi Nagumo would attach to his final bit of operational intelligence. Nagumo commanded the strike force, built around six aircraft carriers, which even now was pounding toward the launch point, some 275 miles northwest of the island of Oahu.

A few hours previously, Consul Kita himself had hurried a final word to Tokyo, concluding: ". . . I imagine in all probability there is considerable opportunity left to take advantage of a surprise attack against these places (the principal bases).

"In my opinion the battleships do not have torpedo nets."[3]

This actually had been intercepted at one of the West Coast monitoring stations and passed along to Washington. However, Army and Navy intelligence baskets were full. It was tossed into a basket tagged for decoding Monday morning.

Now, it was Saturday night in Honolulu and the streets were full of soldiers and sailors "on the town." King Street and Kalakaua Avenue were but a few of the thoroughfares festooned for a tropical version of the Christmas season. At the Naval Receiving Station itself, a long-heralded "Battle of the Bands" promised to keep many sailors on base.

Nonetheless, there were a few in Honolulu tonight who did not share Yoshikawa's relaxed mood. Robert Shivers, twenty-one-year veteran with the F.B.I., was among these exceptions. He had long kept a tap on the telephone lines to both the home of Dr. Mori, the dentist, and to his office.

On Friday evening, Mrs. Mori held a lengthy overseas conversation with the Tokyo newspaper *Yomiuri Shimbun,* costing more than $200. The conversation commenced:

(From Japan) Hello, is this Mori?
(From Honolulu) Hello, this is Mori.
I am sorry to have troubled you. Thank you very much.
Not at all.
I received your telegram and was able to grasp the essential points. I would like to have your impressions on the conditions you are observing at present. Are airplanes flying daily?
Yes, lots of them fly around.
Are they large planes?
Yes, they are quite big.
Are they flying from morning till night?
Well, not to that extent, but last week they were quite active in the air.
I hear there are many sailors there, is that right?
There aren't so many now. There were more in the beginning part of this year and at the ending part of last year.
Is that so?
I do not know why this is so, but it appears that there are very few sailors here at present.
Are any Japanese people there holding meetings to discuss U.S.-Japanese negotiations being conducted presently?

[3]U.S. Naval Institute Proceedings; see Bibliography.

No, not particularly. The minds of the Japanese here appear calmer than expected. . . .

The conversation went on to discuss the lack of "munitions industry" in the Islands, "no factories," the absence of searchlights when "planes fly about at night," the current weather, the fact that "the fleet here seems small" and then final remarks obviously in a personal code about hibiscus and poinsettia flowers as well as food.

The whole rambling discourse bothered Shivers so much when it was decoded Saturday afternoon that he telephoned his friend, Lieutenant Colonel George Bicknell, assistant to Lieutenant Colonel Kendall Fielder, who was General Short's G-2.

"You better come right down here, George," the F.B.I. man asserted.

Bicknell did so immediately, arriving at Shivers' office in the Dillingham Building, on Bishop Street, about 5 P.M. The assistant Army Intelligence officer read the transcript and agreed with his friend. He decided to telephone Colonel Fielder.

"I have a matter of great importance," Bicknell told his superior, "that should be taken up with the general right away!"

Fielder remonstrated that Short was going out to Schofield Barracks for a dinner of the Army Relief Society. Perhaps the commanding general should not be bothered until morning.

Bicknell persisted. It turned out that Fielder, who lived next door to Short on "brass row," was accompanying the Army's Hawaiian Department commander to the affair, along with their wives, who were close friends. Finally, the G-2 officer said he'd go over to the general's residence to talk to him.

Shortly after 5:30 P.M., Fielder called back: "If you can get out to Shafter in ten minutes General Short says he will wait *that* long."

It wouldn't be easy. The streets were crammed with Christmas shoppers and spectators returning from a football game at the University of Hawaii, which was located in the center of the city.

By fast and determined driving, however, Bicknell arrived at Shafter in little more than ten minutes. General Short and Kendall Fielder together read the Mori message.

Fielder preferred to accept the call to the Tokyo newspaper much at its face value, assuming that the Moris were indeed bona fide correspondents. For himself, General Short suggested to Bicknell that he might be "a little too intelligence conscious."

Both the commanding officer and his G-2 chief were anxious to move on to their dinner party amidst the soft lanterns and formalized gentility of the Schofield Officers Club. Short did not care to be out late, especially not tonight, since he must keep a 10 A.M. golf date with Admiral Kimmel on the Fort Shafter links, a regular appointment every other Sunday. Otherwise, the two senior

Japanese propaganda pictures taken during the attack on Pearl Harbor.

NANCIAL PO

he Canadian Newspaper for Businessmen and Investors

irculations   PUBLICATION OFFICE: TORONTO, DECEMBER 13, 1941

ate First Net Pro-
nce 1937; Per-
Best Since 1929

Co. this year will break
ck for the first time since
nancial Post is informed.
net loss in 1940 of over
e appears to ,be a good
a net profit in 1941 of
,000. Such a figure would
profit since 1929 when
$489,454.

st ten months of this year
o. had a gross profit of
million which compared
e over $230,000 for the
a year ago. Bond inte-
first ten months in 1940
0 but it is believed there
moderate reduction in
for the current year, i-
me redemption of the
outstanding bonds. Be-
provision has been
le income taxes for the
onths are understood to
mately four times the
e reported for a year ago
these charges there is in-
the first ten months
of well over $100,000
ss of some $340,000 for the
as of 1940.

nal Months Best

months are usually the
whole Burns year and
ses to be no exception
of what these months
forded by the fact that
ss for the first ten months
s $340,000, the pick-up in

JAPANESE EMBASSY
WASHINGTON

November 25, 1941

Dear Sir:

Referring to the booklet which you
were so kind as to send to me at my request,
I wish to have the articles of the annexed
list delivered to me. I should like to have
them before December 7th at the latest. As
regards the payment, I will be much obliged
if you will designate an agent in Washington,
D.C. (or in New York) to whom I may be able to
pay in cash; this may save me from encounter-
ing many technical difficulties of transfer of
funds under the freezing order.

I may add that the delivery of the
commodities to me will be effected duty free
at the American border. I must, however,
notify the State Department beforehand and
for that purpose I ask you to inform me of the
approximate date of the passage of the goods.

Yours sincerely,

Koto Matsudaira,
First Secretary.

Mr. Herbert S. Mills
Hamilton (Ontario)
Canada

Shows Jap Deadline
Set Long in Advance

Here is a Canadian who has proof that the Jap attack was

From Our Own
MONTREAL.—W
quarters of the firs
represented in per
at the meeting, the
ization of Montrea
put forward by th
the approval of th
te, was approved h
ng majority.

The actual vote o
ed in $14,972,500 of
n favor, with an
in abeyance becau
to validity. Only
were voted against
000 more held
chestionable status
ions were needed
essary three-quarte

Because of the p
to the plan expre
mortgage bondho
headed by C. O. R
anticipated the m
ively. Actually
case. Several hou
by the Ruggles g
various features w
ered important ene
amendment of the
had been largely s
ously published m

Jellett Ans

This singular notice was found in the Toronto Financial
Post two weeks before the attack. The setting of the date,
December 7, appears to have been more than coincidence.

The New York Times

VOL. XCI No. 30,634.   NEW YORK, MONDAY, DECEMBER 8, 1941.   THREE CENTS

JAPAN WARS ON U.S. AND BRITAIN; MAKES SUDDEN ATTACK ON HAWAII; HEAVY FIGHTING AT SEA REPORTED

CONGRESS DECIDED

Roosevelt Will Address It Today and Find It Ready to Vote War

CONFERENCE IS HELD

Legislative Leaders and Cabinet in Sober White House Talk

By C. P. TRUSSELL
Special to THE NEW YORK TIMES

WASHINGTON, Dec. 7.—President Roosevelt will address a joint session of Congress tomorrow and it will find the legislature in a mood to vote on steps he will take to cope with the developments in Pacific.

TOKYO ACTS FIRST

Declaration Follows Air and Sea Attacks on U.S. and Britain

TOGO CALLS ENVOYS

After Fighting Is On, Grew Gets Japan's Reply to Hull Note of Nov. 26

By The Associated Press

TOKYO, Monday, Dec. 8.—Japan went to war against the United States and Britain today with air and sea attacks against Hawaii, followed by a formal declaration of hostilities.

PACIFIC OCEAN: THEATRE OF WAR INVOLVING UNITED STATES AND ITS ALLIES

GUAM BOMBED; ARMY SHIP IS SUNK

U.S. Fliers Head North From Manila— Battleship Oklahoma Set Afire by Torpedo Planes at Honolulu

104 SOLDIERS KILLED AT FIELD IN HAWAII

President Fears 'Very Heavy Losses' on Oahu— Churchill Notifies Japan That a State of War Exists

By FRANK L. KLUCKHOHN
Special to THE NEW YORK TIMES

WASHINGTON, Monday, Dec. 8—Sudden and unexpected attacks on Pearl Harbor, Honolulu, and other United States possessions in the Pacific early yesterday by the Japanese air force and navy plunged the United States and Japan into active war.

JAPANESE FORCE LANDS IN MALAYA

First Attempt Is Repulsed— Singapore Is Bombed and Thailand Invaded

By The Associated Press

SINGAPORE, Monday, Dec. 8.—The Japanese landed in Northern Malaya, 300 miles north of Singapore, today and launched an air raid on this fortress base.

Tokyo Bombers Strike Hard At Our Main Bases on Oahu

By The United Press

HONOLULU, Dec. 7—War broke out with lightning suddenness in the Pacific today when waves of Japanese bombers attacked Hawaii this morning and the United States Fleet struck back with a thunder of big naval rifles.

ENTIRE CITY PUT ON WAR FOOTING

Japanese Rounded Up by FBI, Sent to Ellis Island—Vital Services Are Guarded

HULL DENOUNCES TOKYO 'INFAMY'

Brands Japan 'Fraudulent' in Preparing Attack While Carrying On Parleys

By BERTRAM D. HULEN
Special to THE NEW YORK TIMES

WASHINGTON, Dec. 7—Japan's surprise attack and declaration of war against the United States.

The International Situation

MONDAY, DEC. 8, 1941

Lewis Wins Captive Mine Fight; Arbitrators Grant Union Shop

commanders rarely laid eyes upon one another.

The two bade Bicknell goodnight and left. Frustrated and increasingly worried, Bicknell returned home to Aiea Heights, a few minutes' drive west of Shafter. Deep in thought, he passed the shuttered lights of the Shuncho-ro Restaurant.

The Army now possessed more last-minute intelligence than the Navy, even though its evaluation and portent had been lost on the commanding general. The sea service would wait until morning to read the Mori message, in Shivers' F.B.I. office. Captain Irving H. Mayfield, the Fourteenth Naval District's intelligence officer, advised of the intercept's existence, had gone so far as to phone Commander Edwin T. Layton, the fleet intelligence officer, who would meet with him after Mayfield picked up the message from Shivers.

Layton's particular frustration was his continuing inability to advise Admiral Kimmel on even the approximate location of the Japanese carriers. Just a few days previously, the Pacific Fleet commander, mystified and disturbed, had suggested to Layton, in part facetiously: "Do you mean to say that *they* could be rounding Diamond Head and you wouldn't know it?"

Kimmel had heard the expression "purple" machine for the first time that week when a reference to it had inadvertently appeared in a dispatch from Admiral Stark.

"*What*," the admiral had queried of his intelligence officer in total bafflement, "is a 'purple' machine?"

Layton confessed he had not the slightest idea but would endeavor to find out. There was, indeed, no reason the admiral or General Short should know. There was no "purple" device in all of Hawaii, although General Douglas MacArthur, Commanding General, United States Army Forces in the Far East, had been favored with one of the precious decoders. This lack meant that some significant and often compromising messages from Tokyo, which were known in Washington, were not always relayed to Honolulu. This could have been an oversight.

For example, back in September, Consul Kita had been given a definitive "grid," involving areas and letters of the alphabet, with which he was asked to supply ship anchorage information: for Pearl Harbor, Ford Island, East, West and Middle Loch basins. But this provocative "bit" had no more been relayed to Admiral Kimmel or General Short than had the perplexing "east wind rain" messages.

Saturday turned into early Sunday morning. Station KGMB, instead of signing off at midnight after its usual "Night Owl" program, kept on spinning its records.

Bicknell had been asked to take care of this change from the norm. A flight of twelve B-17's, flying in from Oakland en route to Manila, needed the commercial radio transmission for navigation. The assistant Army intelligence officer did not, however, like the arrangement. He figured that, somehow, it might alert the Japanese, who were at least a potential enemy, to something unusual.

The morning papers were running off Honolulu's web presses somewhat late because of mechanical troubles. An eight-column headline in the *Advertiser* noted: FDR WILL SEND MESSAGE TO EM-PEROR ON WAR CRISIS.

Below it ran a subhead: *Japanese Deny Massing Troops for Thai War*, and below that: *Hirohito Holds Power to Stop Japanese Army*.

It was a typical winter night and early morning in the Islands, with a hint of moisture in the prevailing easterly winds swirling across Kaneohe Bay, the Naval Air Station guarding its entrance, and the Koolau Mountain Range rising skyward beyond the coast.

It had been quiet and routine for the Navy, whose patrol activities had been hampered all year for want of decent ships or planes. Most worthy craft, air or surface, were off in the two task forces or in the Atlantic, which had commanded a naval priority status.

There were only fifty-seven lumbering old PBY's or twin-engined seaplanes, for offshore surveillance. Spare parts were in such short supply that Rear Admiral Claude Bloch, Commandant of the Fourteenth Naval District, decided not to "fritter" any of them away "in distant reconnaissance." So, almost all remained hangared, snug and salt-encrusted in the various air stations. The majority, as a matter of fact, roosted on Ford Island, where the presence of the eight marsupial-like, yet more antiquated battleships afforded a sense of increased protection.

The patrol of coastal sealanes and harbor approach was accomplished by World War I four-stack destroyers. One of them tonight was the *Ward*, 1000 tons and with quite sufficient speed to run away from her own depth charges.

At 3:50 A.M. the *Ward*, at the entrance to Pearl Harbor, received a blinker message from the minesweeper *Condor* that a suspicious object resembling a periscope had been sighted. The destroyer's captain, Lieutenant Commander William W. Outerbridge, sounded general quarters and commenced a search.

For about an hour the *Ward* and *Condor* crisscrossed the approaches to this important channel. Bishop's Point naval radio station, at the harbor entrance, overheard the two captains talking, but did not relay this information to either the Fourteenth Naval District or the Pacific Fleet watch officers. The search was called off without either the *Ward* or *Condor* making a report. Outerbridge lay down in his cabin for a nap.

The sun rose at 6:36. It would be a bright and, for the most part, dry day in the Islands, except for the usual spasmodic showers. At 6:37, Outerbridge was again awakened. There seemed a sense of urgency in the voice of the executive officer, Lieutenant (jg) Oscar Goepner, a reservist recently on active duty.

As the commander raced to the bridge he saw smoke flares being dropped by a PBY overhead and, at the same time, the conning tower of a small submarine, about seventy-five yards distant, trailing the inbound target ship *Antares*. The *Ward* opened fire as it tore forward for a depth charge attack.

About 6:45 the geysers from below, together with oil and some debris in the boiling waters, convinced Outerbridge that he had accounted for the intruder. Now, about 6:50 A.M., he radioed the Fourteenth Naval District: "We have attacked, fired upon and dropped depth charges upon submarine operating in defensive area."

The radioman wrote, then laid aside, the dispatch.

In these same minutes, across the island on its northernmost tip, Kahuku Point, two Signal Corps privates were about to switch off an experimental radar station, employing a new instrument designated "SCR-270B."

Joseph Lockard and George Elliott kept their instrument in operation, however, since they were just "killing time" and for a simple reason. The breakfast truck was late arriving up the tortuous, crushed lava road to this particular promontory, known as Opana.

About 7:02, the Army radar men spotted a sudden shower of "blips" virtually exploding onto the screen. It indicated a large flight of aircraft some 132 miles to the north, maximum receiving range, the direction which Admiral Yarnell had selected for his test nine years previously. Lockard immediately telephoned the radar watch officer, Lieutenant Kermit A. Tyler, at Fort Shafter.

The Air Force lieutenant placed little or no confidence in this unfamiliar electronic "wonder." He also assumed the "blips," if genuine, were impulses caused by the approaching B-17's from California.

"Don't worry about it," Tyler advised.

Lockard and Elliott continued to watch, fascinated, the nearing images on the bright, circular screen until they heard their breakfast transportation driving up through the sugar cane fields towards Opana Point. Now very hungry, they switched off the set and walked out.

During this short interval, another PBY had itself sunk what looked like a second midget submarine a mile off the Pearl Harbor channel.

About 7:15, nearly a half hour after the radio receipt of Outerbridge's attack message, it finally arrived on the desk of the naval district watch officer. At once concerned, he tried to raise someone at fleet headquarters.

His early Sunday morning telephone operator. a Hawaiian woman, spoke almost no English. She couldn't seem to find anyone awake, let alone understand what it was she was supposed to tell them if she did manage to locate them.

The PBY's report of its successful attack was not of much greater use. Contrary to standing orders, the pilot had transmitted in code when he should have employed plain English, so there would be a delay at Pacific Fleet Headquarters while the message was decoded.

Admiral Bloch was reached by the Hawaiian operator, rather surprisingly, before 7:30 and the *Ward* dispatch was read to him by his duty officer. He was not concerned. There had been many false submarine contacts and depth chargings of whales.

Kimmel, up and contemplating his golf match, was informed of the same action about 7:30. His feelings were much the same as Bloch's. He thought he'd obtain some "verification" after breakfast.

Seven minutes later, at 7:37, Admiral Bloch wondered if perhaps the mysterious object might not have been a whale after all. He ordered the destroyer *Monaghan* out of the harbor to sniff around a bit, after which he wanted to make sure that the steel net gates at the harbor entrance were closed.

Nonetheless, the Navy high command on Oahu was better off than the Army's. Neither General Short nor any of his staffers had been informed of these early morning developments.

Even if there had been proper liaison with the Navy, rapid communications between the Army's own posts, staffs, batteries and other units would have been difficult if not impossible this Sunday. The Army had been remodeling its battle command post in an underground location. To protect them against blasting, the Signal Corps had dismantled and moved switchboards, distribution cables and other essential communications gear into remote tunnel locations.

At Schofield Barracks, telephones and central controls linking antiaircraft gun positions had been locked up in an effort to prevent theft and sabotage.

Neither the plot rooms, the firing directors, nor the other essential nerve centers of the fleet at anchor were manned. The officers of the deck kept the keys to ammunition ready boxes.

Waiting for morning colors, at 8:00 A.M., enlisted men lounged under ample deck awnings as a dazzling Pacific sun reflected off the mastheads. Officers who had not gone ashore the past afternoon were at breakfast or still hitting "sack time." In most of the engine rooms, only one boiler was lit, sufficient to run the generators, but scarcely enough to get underway.

Of the seventy combatant ships and twenty-four fleet auxiliaries present in Pearl Harbor and its various lochs, only one was in motion, the three-year-old *Helm,* sweeping slowly over the glassy waters toward the West Loch.

In Washngton, where it was shortly after 1:00 P.M., it was very quiet except at the handsome Japanese embassy on Massachusetts Avenue. There, servants were assisting attachés in a feverish backyard burning of codes and records. Ambassador Nomura and the special envoy, Kurusu, had requested a 1:00 P.M.meeting with Hull, then postponed it until 1:45.

Bratton and Kramer had, before 9:00 A.M., received and decoded the fourteenth part of the message from Tokyo, which announced a breakoff in "further negotiations." Other intercepts set the meeting time, gave further instructions for "machine codes" and all "secret documents," then politely thanked the embassy staff for "your great effort . . . in behalf of our country."

This 1:00 hour, even more than the instructions to burn codes and ciphers, alarmed the Army and Navy intelligence officers—1:00 in the afternoon in Washington was about sunrise at Pearl Harbor.

To those who understood Oriental warfare, the time and the fact that it was Sunday seemed to add up to something which was no less than ominous.

In a panic, Bratton tried to reach General Marshall. He was horseback riding.

Admiral Stark, however, had arrived at his office. The latest dispatches were shown to him somewhat after 10:30 A.M. by his Far Eastern Intelligence Chief, Commander Arthur H. McCollum, to whom Kramer reported.

When the Chief of Naval Operations exhibited not much more excitement than had his Pacific Fleet Commander earlier this morning, to the submarine attack, McCollum urged, "Why don't you pick up the telephone and call Kimmel?"

For a moment, it appeared as though "Betty" Stark would accept McCollum's advice. He took the phone, paused and then said, "No, I think I will call the President."

He tried, but Roosevelt was at the moment having his sinuses drained, which happened almost daily, by the White House physician, Dr. Ross T. McIntire.

While Admiral Stark was mulling over a phone call, Marshall returned to "Quarters A" at Fort Myer and acknowledged Bratton's waiting message. The intelligence officer, emphasizing the importance of what he had to show him, offered to hurry across the Potomac to the Chief of Staff's home.

Marshall said "no," he was coming to his office anyhow.

Arriving about 11:25, he was immediately given the "one o'clock message." He read it aloud in the presence of Bratton and other staffers for a full fifteen minutes, ignoring periodic attempts to interrupt him.

Finally, he observed there probably was "some definite significance" to the dispatch. Then he took a pencil and deliberately wrote a message which he proposed to send to Hawaii, Panama, the Philippines and perhaps some other outposts: "The Japanese are presenting at 1 P.M. Eastern Standard Time today what amounts to an ultimatum. Also they are under orders to destroy their code machine immediately. Just what significance the hour set may have we do not know, but be on alert accordingly."

Marshall next telephoned Admiral Stark and told him what he was doing. The Chief of Naval Operations replied that he did not consider "any additional warning . . . necessary."

However, the Chief of Staff had barely replaced his receiver when the Admiral rang back and requested that a phrase be added to the warning, "inform the Navy."

At 11:50 A.M. General Marshall gave the message to Bratton to deliver to the Signal Corps for immediate coding and transmission.

"Immediate," it turned out, would be thirty or forty minutes.

Actually, the communication arrived in the commercial RCA offices in Honolulu at about the time Admiral Kimmel was asking for "verification" of the depth-charging. The clerk handed it to a motorcycle messenger and told him to take it out to Fort Shafter when he was ready.

There was never a question of telephoning, either at the Honolulu cable office or by General Marshall himself. The Chief of Staff would later explain that he disliked to use a telephone "scrambler" because he believed that German agents were able to "unscramble."

At almost the same time, 7:40 A.M., when the Japanese messenger boy was starting on his mission, far swifter machines had picked up Oahu's shining coastline: forty torpedo bombers, forty-nine high-level bombers, fifty-one dive bombers and fifty-one fighters. All of them were of the latest design, carrying the newest armament, and—splashed under wing tips were the glaring red circles of the Rising Sun.

CHAPTER 5

There was almost no reaction to the arrival of the Japanese attack force over Oahu. The aircraft swept above Kahuku Point, even as Lockard and Elliott were being trundled down to breakfast, then separated into four principal waves on either side of the Waianae Range, and headed generally south and east.

Those on the island who looked up at them entertained no doubts that this was another Navy and/or Air Force exercise. The few who noticed the red circles under the wings rationalized that they were some form of camouflage.

A lifeguard, preparing for a routine Sunday at the Barber's Point Military Reservation, on the southwest tip of Oahu, watched a low-flying plane offshore pass over a freighter, followed by a column of water geysering in its wake. Next a bomb appeared to explode a few hundred yards up the beach.

He thought to himself that such war "exercises" were "very dangerous for the swimmers."

The surprising aspect, in addition to the unfamiliar design of the swift intruders, was that there were so many of them. When, indeed, would nearly two hundred American aircraft have been massed in close formation?

The Army's entire Hawaiian Air Force totalled not many more than this. In addition, all United States planes were equipped with retractable wheels unlike the "down" gear of the Japanese.

The time was now 7:55 A.M.

Golfers on the island's several links glanced up and went on with their game. Most churchgoers, conscious of the roar of engines overhead, just kept on their way.

The first strafing run—by a matter of seconds—probably was made on Kaneohe Naval Air Station. It was all the way across the island on the east coast. Seemingly, tactical preference would have been accorded Schofield Barracks and Wheeler Field, closer and almost due south from Kahuku Point.

A workboat load of sailors moving across Kaneohe Bay was directly in line as an echelon of the planes started no more than fifty feet across the water toward the air strip and hangars.

"Here comes Tojo!" one of the sailors laughed.

Aviation Machinist Mate First Class Otto Horky from Staunton, Illinois, was adjusting a PBY engine when he saw "a brightly polished fighter plane from nowhere and his machine gun tracers plowing into one of the PBY's in the water. 'Why that drunken S.O.B. . . .' went through all our minds, [we were] so sure that it was an Air Force man with alcohol stored elsewhere than his de-icer tank."

But when the fighter plane pulled out of its dive, the pilot "winged over as though in extreme joy" and Horky saw the rising sun.

"The PBY blew up into a tall column of red fire and black smoke. Like a covey of quail, the group I was with broke and ran for the seaplane ramps about five hundred feet distant."

In seconds, the seamen in the workboat didn't think anything was funny. Some jumped for their lives. For others, it was already too late.

A cook, Joseph Burghard, of Ventura, California, walked out of the galley of Naval Mobile Base Hospital No. 2, Pearl Harbor, to watch "the return of the patrol planes." Then he saw the "red circle on their wings" and they commenced to dive.

Rear Admiral William R. Furlong, aboard the old minelayer *Oglala*, his flagship, moored near the drydock, recognized those red "meatballs." As senior officer present "afloat" among the ships now in the area, he ordered the signal hoisted: "All ships in harbor sortie!"

This was far more easily commanded than effected.

At 7:58, the signal tower on the naval base, all but brushed by a low-flying plane, telephoned to Pacific Fleet Headquarters, which at once broadcast to "all ships in the Hawaiian area": "Air raid on Pearl Harbor! This is no drill!"

An alert radioman at the Mare Island Navy Station, San Francisco, picked up this local transmission from 2200 miles away and relayed it at once to Washington. President Roosevelt was informed about 1:40 P.M., even as the Japanese envoys were en route to the State Department to deliver the fourteen-point message, already known to its recipients.

Tai Sing Loo, a civilian photographer at the Naval Base, had matters of no greater moment on his mind than to snap some background for his personal Christmas card. He would write, "I was great shock with surprise the war are on. . . ."[4]

4U.S. Naval Institute Proceedings; see Bibliography.

The torpedo planes were swooping now.

On the *Arizona*, flying the flag of Battleship Division One, Major Alan Shapley, of the Marine detachment, was in the process of rounding up the vessel's baseball team when suddenly he found himself lifted and thrown heavily onto the deck. He thought, for some reason, that a crane had fallen.

When he picked himself up and struggled to the nearest opened hatch, he saw that the cause of the concussion was no broken crane—but "a sky filled with planes." He could not know that an aerial torpedo had driven home slightly aft of No. 1 gun turret, below the waterline.

Bells and horns were sounding their deafening reveille in response to someone's pulling a general quarters alarm. And Shapley already was seized with "a hopeless sort of feeling."

On the *Nevada*, next in line, came snatches of the National Anthem through the din of explosions and shouts. Strafed once, the band doggedly stuck through morning colors to a shaky end.

Less stoic, the "Catholic Church party" just summoned to "lay up to" the quarter of the cruiser *Phoenix*, broke for their gun stations.

Within the relatively greater sanctuary of an inner mooring slip, Yeoman Third Class Everett Johnson aboard the flagship USS *Argonne*, an old submarine tender, looked out of a porthole in the communications office to see a hangar on Ford Island burning briskly.

"Well, this is it," Johnson observed anticlimactically.

Like many other ships, the heavy cruiser *New Orleans* was without electricity. In the haste to cast her loose, a seaman had chopped through the "hot" electric cable to shore. There was insufficient steam to start her own generators.

As the men moved ammunition through darkened shafts to the guns via human chains, the Reverend Howell Forgy, the cruiser's chaplain, exhorted, "Praise the Lord, and pass the ammunition!" Since he was a man of the cloth, the Presbyterian minister could not personally serve the guns.

Seemingly, all of the battleships were pummelled within the first ten minutes of the attack. The *Oklahoma* took three torpedoes on her port side and started to list at once, with the tortured creaks and rasplike groans of some dying monster. All 1354 men on board could not feel other than a premonition of certain, implacable doom. Shipping water, she keeled so rapidly that the several hundred caught below in the cavernous 1916-class "dreadnought" could hardly grope to safety, much less beat to their battle stations.

Pay clerk, D. L. Westfall, who had been shaving, started for his station in radio central.

"As I was passing along the third deck up a port ammunition

passageway," he would recall, "I felt two more hits. The lights went out in the passageway except for one battle light and two panel lights in the boat crane machinery space.

"By the time I reached the compartment abreast the armory, the ship had picked up a 10-15 degree list to port. There were a couple of battle lights on in this compartment. Water and oil were bubbling up along the junction of the bulkhead and deck of the electrical workshop, portside. Repair parties were busy closing watertight doors."

Lieutenant Commander William M. Hobby, Jr., the second in seniority aboard the *Oklahoma*, was soon directing the flooding of the starboard blisters, the equivalent to those on port which had already belied their function as torpedo bulwarks.

"Streams of men were pouring up through hatches to the topside," he wrote. "A second or so later at about the time I was back down to the main deck aft again, came the fourth torpedo hit, and the ship continued to list to port—at least a twenty-degree list at this time, I estimate, and still listing. I directed petty officers near me to spread out over the length of the ship and keep the men as orderly and calm as possible. I sighted Commander Jesse L. Kenworthy (the executive officer) on the starboard catwalk and made my way to him and told him that I thought the best now was to save as many men as possible, that it was now impossible to make further watertight closures and establish any further watertight integrity. He agreed and we both passed the word to abandon ship. I called to men on main deck aft.

"Although there were now hundreds of men on the starboard side, the general conduct of all hands was quiet and calm. There was an explosion around the port side of the forecastle, which I thought was a bomb hit. I worked my way forward and Commander Kenworthy worked his way aft. There was another shock and concussion and vibration and fuel oil splashed in streams over everything topside. This was either another torpedo hit or a large bomb hit close aboard. The ship continued to list over to port, now about thirty degrees, or more, I thought. I entered #1 casemate to see about the escape of men from below to topside. Men were still coming out through casemates, and thence out through gun ports to the catwalk and onto the side."

It was every man for himself. By 8:01, one could walk across the starboard side without leaning against what had been a slope.

The *West Virginia*, known to her crew as "Wee Vee," moored astern of the luckless *Oklahoma*, swallowed six, possibly seven torpedoes and two special 15- or 16-inch armor-piercing bombs. An alert ensign, as officer of the deck, saved lives by ordering, when he saw the first plane attack Ford Island: "Away fire and rescue party!"

Thus, many who were below rushed to their stations topsides. The "Wee Vee," along with the *Nevada*, had been among the first ships to

U.S.S. West Virginia and U.S.A. Arizona aflame, the keel, of the capsized U.S.S. Oklahoma is at extreme left.

The U.S.S. Shaw exploding.

Two views of Pearl Harbor immediately after the attack.

WORLD WIDE PHOTO

Oil burning on water near Naval Air Station boat landing.

The U·S·S. Shaw in floating drydock after the attack.

The capsized U.S.S. Utah with the U.S.S. Raleigh in the background.

U.S.S. Vestal, twice bombed by Japanese fliers, was beached after the ship started flooding.

Center background, in the drydock destroyers Cassin and Downes are burning. Also in the drydock is the battleship Pennsylvania. Alongside the pier are the cruiser Helena, listing slightly from a torpedo hit, and the capsized minelayer Oglala.

Pumps are rapidly clearing the Maryland (foreground) of
water, while the West Virginia and Tennessee still burn.
The keel of the Oklahoma, which turned turtle, is at right.

Two years later the Oglala was righted, repaired and placed back in commission.

The capsized minelayer Oglala.

A young visitor looks across Pearl Harbor from the Arizona Monument, which is built on top of the sunken battleship.

ARMY TIMES PHOTO

The Arizona Monument as it appears today.

return fire, relatively ineffective as were the principal 3-inch and 1.1-inch antiaircraft batteries.

However, the *West Virginia* was listing so heavily to port that it was necessary for each ammunition passer to be held more or less upright by a second man. Something had to be done.

Lieutenant Claude V. Ricketts, a gunnery officer, who organized counter-flooding wrote: "Wounded were being brought up the hatches forward. The ship was now listing so heavily that on the linoleum decks it was impossible to walk without holding onto something.

"I reached the third deck by the ladder at frame 87 starboard and went forward to the first group of counterflooding valves. . .

"I went to the antiaircraft battery on the boat deck and found that all ammunition from the ready boxes had been expended. I went to 'Times Square' and formed an ammunition train, opening hatches as necessary."

The *West Virginia* settled the few feet down to a muddy bottom, enabling guns on both sides to continue firing in spite of the flames and black smoke still pouring from her midsection. A bomb, which had landed on the No. 2 turret of her mooring mate, the *Tennessee*, sent a storm of fragments in all directions, shredding the bridge of the *West Virginia*.

Captain Mervyn Bennion, who had expressed pride in the struggle to keep his ship in action, was hit by shrapnel. Slumped across a doorsill, the mortally wounded fifty-four-year-old commander of the *West Virginia* kept asking two junior officers how the fight was "going." Lieutenant Ricketts wrote of his dying captain, "Although in great pain, he kept inquiring about the condition of the ship, whether or not we had any pumps running,etc. He was particularly concerned about the fires on board and the oil on the surface of the water."

While at first it appeared that the little repair ship *Vestal*, moored alongside the *Arizona*, was for some perverse reason being meted more attention by the enemy than the "battlewagon," at about 8:00 an armor-piercing bomb crashed through her deck into the forward powder magazine.

Still staring, as if hypnotized, in front of the mobile hospital, Joseph Burghard watched "huge flames" suddenly shooting skyward from the *Arizona*. At once he realized the battleship had received her "death blow." Others ashore could swear she seemed to "leap out of the water."

Shapley, the Marine officer, was blown into the harbor. Numbed, he nonetheless struck out for Ford Island, stroking through an ever-thickening oil slick. On his way, he managed to assist two shipmates.

D.A. Graham, an aviation machinist's mate first class, watched "lots of men coming out on the quarterdeck with every stitch of clothing and shoes blown off, painfully burned and shocked. Mr. Fuqua [Lieutenant Commander Samuel G. Fuqua] was the senior officer on deck and set an example for the men by being unperturbed, calm, cool and collected, exemplifying the courage and traditions of an officer under fire. It seemed as if the painfully burned and shocked men were inspired and took things in stride when they saw Mr. Fuqua standing on the quarterdeck, unconcerned about the bombing and strafing.

"There was no going to pieces or growing panicky noticeable, and he directed the moving of the wounded and burned men who were on the quarterdeck to the motor launches and boats. He gave orders to get the life rafts on #3 barbette down, supervised the loading of the casualties, assisted by a younger officer, Ensign J.D. Miller, who set a very good example by being cool, calm, and collected.

"The signal gang, quartermasters and all hands on the bridge went up—as the signalmen were trying to put out a fire in the signal rack and grabbing signal flags out to hoist a signal, the whole bridge went up, flames enveloping and obscuring them from view as the flames shot upward twice as high as the tops. A bomb hit on the starboard side of the stern 5-inch gun and antiaircraft gun, and got most of the Marine crew and antiaircraft crew and came down through the casemate and executive officer's office.

"After the big explosion and 'swish' the men, painfully burned and wounded, dazed beyond comprehension, came out on the quarterdeck. I had to stop some of them from entering the flames later on and directed them over to the starboard side of the deck to the gangway for embarking, encouraging them to be calm."

Not so fortunate were more than 1200 officers and men, of the some 1550 on board. They died along with their ship. Among them were Admiral Isaac C. Kidd, commanding Battleship Division One, and Captain Franklin Van Valkenburgh, the *Arizona*'s commanding officer, who had never left the bridge. (Both, along with Captain Bennion, received the Medal of Honor posthumously.)

Even so, the Stars and Stripes still flew from *Arizona*'s blackened, tilting superstructure, and several machine guns continued to bang away through the furiously burning shambles.

The blast virtually wrecked her outboard neighbor, the *Vestal*, and tossed the skipper, Commander Cassin Young, overboard. Even though the executive officer had then ordered abandon ship, the captain proved indestructible of will and body. He swam back and found the *Vestal* afloat. By chance, a Navy tug came by, took a line and towed the repair ship to the northern shore of the harbor, under fire all the while.

Next, the planes seemed to turn on the *California*. Still encouraging his gunners on the *New Orleans*, Chaplain Forgy watched a "Jap dive-bomber gliding down toward Battleship Row. He seemed to be loafing in, deliberately taking his time to pick out just what he wanted to hit.

"I couldn't take my eyes off him. I followed him down until I saw the bombs drop out of his belly. Sticking out of the cockpit was the helmeted head of the Jap pilot. There was something mocking about the big rising-sun balls under the wings of the plane.

"They were coming down for the big battleship *California*. The bombs hit her amidships, right by the stacks. A flash, fire and smoke jumped into the air all at once.

"The Jap opened his throttle wide and raced away from his victim with a terrific roar. Now our guns began thundering in my ears. The sky all around the plane was laced with streaming trails of tracers. The Jap couldn't get through that stuff—but he did.

"More planes came, one after another with a sort of abandon, they floated by in slow, aggravating glides, right through the very center of our noisy barrage of AA fire."

The 1909-vintage battleship *Utah*, used as an aerial target ship, moored on the opposite side of Ford Island, was heavily bombed probably because she occupied a berth usually reserved for an aircraft carrier. Two underwater hits had flooded the engine room and opened up her old seams.

She started to keel over very quickly. The two layers of 6-$\times$-12-foot timbers, used to protect crewmen during target practice, fell and splintered, causing many casualties. These, too, might have suggested an aircraft carrier's deck to the Japanese.

Chief Water Tender Peter Tomish insisted on one more look in the engine spaces even though it was obvious the *Utah* was capsizing. Shipmates were insistent that he could not possibly return topside.

"Gotta get below to my men," he replied, "and my boilers or they'll blow to hell!"

The boilers did not "blow to hell," but the old battleship did turn onto her side shortly after 8:10. Austrian-born Tomish, even as he had been warned, never came up again. (Tomish, too, was awarded the Medal of Honor, the only member of the *Utah*'s last crew to be so honored.)

The pall of smoke rising from the ships as well as the flaming oil on the water now funnelled up and joined with that from Ford Island where thirty-three of the seventy Navy planes, PBY's and single-engine patrol and bombing types were already being reduced to twisted metal and ashes.

At Ewa, a Marine Corps air base, near West Loch, planes were also going up in flames—almost all the fifty fighters located there. However, plucky Marines got some of the machine guns into action, firing in completely exposed positions. One even kept discharging his service pistol skyward.

Among them, a master technical sergeant who was a veteran of World War I was ordered by an officer, "Take cover!"

"To hell with the cover!" the sergeant yelled back. "I'm fifty years old. Get the kids under cover!"

Yet with all the reckless bravery, only four died at Ewa.

At adjacent Hickam Field, petroleum storage tanks and hangars were burning furiously. Thirty-five Air Corps enlisted men at breakfast died after a direct bomb hit on their barracks, named "Hale Makai."

The majority of the Air Corpsmen were so sleepy after their Saturday night that it was all but impossible to convey a sense of urgency and to get them in motion. Roger S. Moran, for example, assigned to ordnance duties with the 5th Bombardment Group of B-18's, had to wake up a buddy twice to convince him that Hickam was under attack.

"I was 'nutty,' he kept telling me," Moran recalled, "until finally I showed him the billowing cloud of black smoke outside the window. Then I could hardly get him to wait long enough to pull on his pants to report to his bomb service truck."

Bombs landed on the guardhouse, putting the air raid siren out of order and on the ordnance building, delaying access to "ready" ammunition. Other missiles also hit machine shops, hangars, the theater, the parade ground, the post exchange, even the "Snake Ranch," a beer garden. The baseball diamond was pockmarked in an area where outdated maps carried by the Japanese showed gasoline storage tanks. Planes, lined up with only ten feet between wingtips, were a total loss. Luckily, the longest runways in the Islands were missed.

Families, not waiting for orders, were abandoning their extensive living areas, heading in cars, on bicycles or on foot for the main gates and, presumably, the rugged fringing hills. A few had friends or relatives in Honolulu which at the moment appeared to be a much safer place. Whether or not it actually was any safer, the citizenry had very little cause for reassurance.

The family of Lieutenant (jg) Herbert R. Tucker, a Navy diver, hastily improvised an air raid shelter in a neighbor's kitchen. Both were quartered in a section of the submarine base known as Makalapa Court. While the husbands raced to their duty stations, the wives heaped mattresses atop chairs and tables, under which the children munched jelly sandwiches and wondered why their parents were so worried.

"The streets," wrote Harry Stroup for the *Advertiser*, "were lined from one end of the city to the other with men, women and children, some still in their pajamas and night shirts. All were looking westward, most of them with a somewhat perplexed expression on their faces. . . ."

Although the radio had already unrealistically advised: "Keep off the streets! Keep off the streets! Don't use the telephone!"

Tai Sing Loo, the base photographer, had his own reasons for agreeing with this admonition even though it was his job to make pictures, no matter the hazards.

"So, I'm afraid," he would observe, "someone will make a mistake me as a Jap and shot me down. . . ."

For the spy, Ensign Yoshikawa, the first minutes of this Sunday morning attack had already been his tour de force. "I was at breakfast," he would write, "at 0755 when the first bomb fell at Pearl Harbor. Still somewhat befuddled by my late work on the previous night, I thought it probably a maneuver but rose and switched on the shortwave radio."

He had heard, before hurrying over to the consulate for breakfast, on the 8 A.M. news from Tokyo: "east wind rain." As the prearranged code had translated, U.S.-Japanese relations were indeed "in danger."

CHAPTER 6

A wave of fighter planes swept through Kole Kole Pass in the Waianae Ridge at 8:07 o'clock to pounce on Wheeler, a fighter base next to Schofield.

"All hell broke loose," recalled Thomas Dowds, of Pittsburgh, with the Third Engineers at Schofield Barracks. "I was getting ready to go to Mass, had just taken a shower and was standing at the window on the third floor of the barracks. At first I thought it was some kind of maneuver or something.

"I saw the planes but I could not make out the insignia due to the morning sun hitting me in the eyes. I heard the explosions and felt the concussion coming through the screen. Then I heard the call to arms and hit for my locker, starting to get into uniform, full field pack, rifle, helmet, gas mask. . . . I still did not know that we were under attack."

When Dowds fell into formation in front of the Third Engineers barracks, he soon *did* know what was happening. The captain informed his company that the United States was at war. He had, in fact, anticipated the formal declaration by one day.

"I cannot explain the feeling that came over me," Dowds continued. "The men from Wheeler were running over to our area calling for help. Some were wounded slightly, some ran so far and dropped in their tracks. The war already had ended for those."

Corporal Harold Cook, a New Englander, had returned to the 27th Infantry Regiment compound at Schofield, following antisabotage patrol and was leaving the mess hall when he heard "the roar of planes, bombs exploding and much bewilderment." Cook, who was about to return to the mainland, said, "Machine gun bullets started flying all around us. Scattering for what cover there was, we were informed that the Japanese were attacking Pearl Harbor, Wheeler and Hickam

Fields—and us, along with other positions on the island.

"We were all told to draw weapons and ammo and keep under cover. Men were firing machine guns, cradled in their arms, at the oncoming planes. Many of these men were severely injured by the overheated weapons.

"A major posted me with only a .45 caliber pistol to patrol the quadrangle. Imagine, trying to conceal myself behind a lamp post about six inches square and firing a .45 at planes! Well, I did."

Mrs. Frank T. Ostenberg, a colonel's wife, lived in "officers' country" on the Wheeler base.

"We were up early that Sunday morning," she recalled, "to take turns going to church as our maid had the day off. First I had the children—Jane, four, and Tom, one—fed, and while giving the younger child his breakfast, we heard a terrible explosion. My husband and I looked at each other wondering what had happened. I asked if the Navy could be having target practice on Sunday morning when suddenly another explosion, worse than the first, shook the doors and everything in the house. We heard planes flying low overhead.

"As we looked out the windows we could see huge billows of smoke rising from the hangars. My husband identified the planes as Jap planes and told me the awful truth; that the Japanese were attacking us and we would now be at war.

"I was frozen in my tracks and held my two children close to my side. The bombing was getting worse and then machine gunning, several bullets hitting our house.

"We dressed as quickly as possible. My husband told me to keep away from the windows and then left us while he drove off through the strafing to alert the regiment stationed a few miles away at Schofield Barracks.

"He had no sooner gone when there was a knock at our door. Four Air Force officers with their wives had left their two-story apartment building and had run across the field to our house for protection, we, having a double roof on our house, one flat concrete roof and a wooden gable one.

"They told me how they had all been knocked to the ground on the way over; fortunately none of them was hurt.

"The officers left their wives with me, for which I was very thankful, not to have to be alone, and they went off to get their planes.

"Shortly, the four officers returned saying that all American planes had been destroyed and there was nothing with which to fight. They took their wives back to their apartments to get dressed so they would be ready to move to safer surroundings, if there were any.

"Again I was left alone with my two children. Then the phone rang; it was my husband calling to say they were sending a truck to pick us up, along with other wives and children of the regiment who lived nearby.

"On the way to regimental headquarters, we saw frenzied activity. Men in undershirts were strapping pistols on their hips and feverishly setting up machine guns in protected places. There was much shouting of orders and blowing of whistles but the air raid siren never did sound. Women and children stood outside staring in disbelief at the planes in the sky. It is remarkable that not a single dependent in the big Schofield Barracks area was hit despite the strafing attacks on fully exposed persons."

Cook, in the meantime, had been ordered from behind his lamp post to load up a truck with barbed wire and an antitank gun, a useless weapon at the moment, and head for Fort Shafter, "down the long isolated Kamehameha Highway."

The corporal "tore the governor off the vehicle's motor and took off through Wheeler Field. The sergeant who accompanied me was firing his Browning automatic rifle continuously.

"Wheeler was in a shambles, dead and wounded everywhere. Jap planes strafed us the whole thirty-three miles of our trip. Military police were stationed at every intersection urging all to speed up.

"Speeding past Pearl City we could see the bombings, smoke, explosions and twisted masses of steel and ships at Pearl Harbor."

Other people were racing from Wheeler. Two P-40 pilots from the small Haleiwa fighter strip, on the northwest coast, Lieutenants George Welch and Ken Taylor, had been finishing up an all-night poker game.

A phone call to Haleiwa elicited the remarkable intelligence that the enemy had apparently overlooked this field and the P-40's were still unscathed. A one hundred-mile-an-hour dash in Taylor's car hastened the pair to Haleiwa in five minutes. They had been airborne only seconds when Welch shot down a two-man dive bomber, and Taylor accounted for a second enemy plane.

At Wahiawa, a cluster of homes across the road from the Schofield-Wheeler complex, two planes strafed the streets, up and down. The pilots conceivably thought these were military byways leading into the twin bases. A lieutenant and a sergeant at a nearby communications outpost grabbed two automatic rifles and kept firing.

One of their attackers soared upward and flew off. The pair watched the second vanish over a hill, giving them the impression it was going to crash.

An elderly Japanese resident of Wahiawa arrived breathless at the Wheeler gate to gasp, accusingly, "Hey, wassamatta, you? Bomb my house! You wanna play bomb, bomb *your* place!"

Officers, enlisted, civilians on duty at the island's many posts and

B-17 Flying Fortresses, probably among those that flew in from the West Coast during the attack, on Hickam Field.

Oil fires burn out of control at Hickam Field.

US ARMY PHOTO

The attack over, Marine gunners and sentries relax on their parade ground within the Naval Base complex. The smoke is coming from the burning battleships.

The seaplane ramp on Ford Island immediately after the attack. The masts and stack in the background belong to the Nevada, grounded after making an unsuccessful dash for the open sea.

The only P-40 on the island today is this mockup prepared for a motion picture of the attack.

Three P-40's which attempted to take off from Bellows Field, were shot down immediately. Most of the twelve P-40's there, lined up in neat rows, were riddled by machine guns like this one.

Gunnery under attack.

The remains of a single-engine plane at Hickam Field.

US planes damaged during the attack.

The wreckage of a Navy PBY at Bellows Field.

Clouds of smoke billow from Hickam Field behind "Officers' Country."

"Officers' Country" today.

stations, caught at home, were all throwing on their clothes preparatory to reporting "on the double."

One of them, Lieutenant (jg) Victor J. Niiranen, a young dental officer from Minnesota, had been recently assigned to the *Utah*. He would have been aboard Saturday night except that he had just welcomed his wife from the States to a beach cottage he had rented in Kuhio.

Informed of the attack by telephone, he picked up the ship's captain, Lieutenant Commander James Steele, and arrived at the naval base about 8:35. Niiranen soon realized that his cabin, amidship, had been demolished by the first torpedo. His roommate was missing.

Meanwhile, the *Oklahoma*, too, was beyond recall. She had completed her roll and was lying on her side like a monstrous beached whale. One propeller, shaft and all, protruded incongruously above the water.

Commander Hobby had himself climbed up through a gun port and "out over the side. The ship was capsizing and the angle was about ninety degrees. I pulled myself along the side and bottom as the vessel keeled over; the ship settled when the mast and stack apparently hit bottom, with an angle of approximately 145 degrees, starboard side uppermost.

"I sat on the bottom at about frame 60; hundreds of men were along the hull making their way to the water's edge."

More than four hundred men were still inside he battleship, including Chief Machinist W.F. Staff, trapped in the forward air compressor room, along with an electrician's mate and a fireman.

"When the lights went out," Staff wrote, "the fireman and electrician's mate started to go out a hatch which had been closed; they were yelling and screaming. Water and fuel oil were coming down the hatch. I tried to stop them from opening the hatch but I couldn't.

"The next thing we knew we were all under water and oil. It took us some time in the dark to find out that we were back in A-28 and the ship had capsized. We then tried to get into the linen storeroom. It was on the starboard side and was out of the water. A-28 (the compressor room) was about half full of oil and water. The storeroom was locked and it took several hours to beat the lock off with a wrench that we found on the air compressor. We could not get into the storeroom as gear must have wedged against the door.

"We tried to get into a small storeroom which was on the overhead, but it was also locked and we could not position ourselves to beat the lock off."

Ensign Richard L. Stewart, of Memphis, a June graduate of Annapolis, wouldn't have been aboard the drydocked *Downes* at all had not his car broken down the night before. There was no convenient way to go anywhere else. The destroyer was beside the *Cassin* and directly in front of the battleship *Pennsylvania*, all under repair.

Stewart, whose duty station was in the engine room, had been awakened by what he thought was the ship slipping off her keel blocks. He pulled on his dungarees and white dress shoes, since they were the closest pair, and ran on deck.

"It didn't take long to find out what was going on," he recalled. She was rolling off her keel blocks and facing even greater damage as the planes dived at her again and again. As a matter of fact, Stewart had been mentally prepared for something like this, so much so that he had left his heirloom watch at home on his previous month's leave.

Crewmen had already put essential elements of a 5-inch 38-caliber gun, taken down for an overhaul, back together and were banging off a few rounds. Stewart raced to his own 50-caliber gun station aft and soon had his men firing skyward.

"We were pretty well frustrated," he noted, "because of danger of hitting the *Pennsylvania* (already damaged by one bomb) right behind us and looking about as big as a mountain."

By 8:30 there was a lull in the skies. The planes had disappeared.

The fleet oiler *Neosho*, half-loaded with aviation gasoline and warped against a fuel dock just ahead of the capsized *Oklahoma*, cut her lines and used the period of calm to ease out of the channel. She had not been scratched but her luck did not last much longer. She was torpedoed in the Coral Sea in May, 1942, with a heavy loss of life.

At the same time, the *Nevada*, low in the water after one torpedo and two bomb hits, accomplished the remarkable by getting under way, with the harbor mouth her goal. She was able to move under her own power only because of a stroke of good luck. Steam had been raised on a second boiler earlier in the morning with the intention of switching the generator boilers.

At approximately 8:35, a small Japanese submarine was found inside the harbor, having apparently moved through the nets when they were opened earlier to allow the minesweeper *Condor* to leave and the *Antares* to enter. It was rammed and sunk by the *Monaghan* after several Navy vessels opened fire upon it.

At this time, a group of eighteen planes off the *Enterprise*, heading home from Wake and nearly two hundred miles west of Oahu, ran into the worst luck they had ever experienced. On general reconnaissance duty ahead of the carrier, they were due to land at Ford Island, where they would be serviced and then flown or hoisted back aboard the *Enterprise*, possibly the next morning.

The first intimation that all was not well was when the pilots caught over earphones the anguished cry from one of their number, Ensign Manuel Gonzales, "Don't shoot! I'm a friendly plane!" He was never heard from again.

One plane turned back, found that the *Enterprise,* by now alerted to the Pearl Harbor invasion, had gone on radio silence, altered course and vanished. The pilot finally crash-landed in a field on Kaui.

Another ground-looped to a halt on Ford Island through a murderous burst of Navy fire. Another landed at Ewa, only to be waved off again. One was shot down by U.S. anti-aircraft fire over the ocean, although both the flier and rear gunner were ultimately rescued. Three more planes in addition to Gonzales' were destroyed by the Japanese. Only one pilot survived.

Three miles from land, Lieutenant (jg) Clarence Dickinson, with a Scouting 6, spotted a 4-engined patrol bomber, which he knew wasn't "friendly." Then four or five Zeroes made a pass. His rear gunner and radioman, W.C. Miller, commenced firing.

"Mr. Dickinson, I have been hit once," Miller in the next instant called over the intercom, "but I think I have got one of them."

Sure enough, as the pilot looked out, an enemy appeared to be spiralling seaward.

"Are you all right, Miller?" Dickinson asked.

"Mr. Dickinson," came the reply, "I've expended six cans of ammunition."

Next, there issued an "agonized" scream from the back cockpit. Dickinson, fighting the plane's stick, rudder elevators and ailerons, soon realized his controls had been shot away. After the pilot had repeatedly called to Miller without response, he concluded his gunner must be dead.

He opened the cowl, and jumped. Luck was with Dickinson. He landed in a dirt bank near Ewa.

Other planes from the *Enterprise*'s ill-fated morning patrol managed to land on Ewa or Ford Island. Dickinson joined his shipmates to wait while their planes were fueled as a prelude to combat.

The B-17's, for which KGBM had been broadcasting all night, were also coming in during this time. Without guns they couldn't even defend themselves as the carrier's group had. The lead bombers to pick up Diamond Head had mistaken the Japanese planes, close by, for escorts. Then, the pilots heard the Hickam tower warn that the field was under attack by "unidentified enemy planes."

Low in gas, their crews exhausted from the overnight flight, the bombers had to get down. The first one touched the runway of Hickam, afire. It had been hit. By the time the 4-engined bomber had rolled to a stop it was cracking in half. The entire crew raced to safety, except for the flight surgeon, who was killed by strafers.

The other B-17's were luckier. One made it to Wheeler, another to the tiny airstrip at Haleiwa, one on a golf course and still another flopped wheels-up onto Bellows Field, on the east coast. There were wounded aboard.

The arrival of this big plane was the first direct effect of war to be felt at Bellows. Things then picked up. Attracted partly by the sight of the crippled bomber on the runway, Japanese fighters peeled out of the clouds and screamed down.

Tents were strafed, waking up Corporal Clarence McKinley, of the signal section, among others. These unfriendly visitors were particularly disturbing since, as McKinley admitted, he "hadn't any plane recognition at that time."

However, an acting first sergeant prodded McKinley and his tent mates out of bed and to the armament building to draw automatic rifles and machine guns. No one could find belts for the machine gun cartridges or clips that would substitute.

Then, for want of something better to do, the men were ordered to "disperse wherever we wanted, in ditches, behind buildings and in open spaces." By McKinley's assessment: "The firepower we could bring to bear at this time consisted of small arms held by the casual detachment and one machine gun on an old observation plane, belonging to the 86th Observation Squadron. We took positions as best we could."

Then, at 8:45 A.M., the second wave of hostile planes roared over Oahu.

CHAPTER 7

Miss Betty Marrs, a Red Cross nurse, who had been listening from the porch of her home in Waikiki to the distant explosions from the first wave of the attack, now saw the second sweeping by a few minutes before 9:00 A.M. Then two shells hit the water just offshore and detonated.

"I knew this wasn't foolin'," she told herself as she hurried into uniform.

Mrs. Thomas J. Nixon, III, wife of a Navy junior lieutenant aboard the *Lexington*, was reading the Sunday funnies spread out before her on the floor of her Waikiki apartment. When she heard the concussions from the bombing she at once recalled a conversation of a few nights before when her husband suggested an attack on Pearl Harbor was "strategically impossible."

When she looked out of the window and saw a smouldering bomb crater in the street, she decided that maybe it had become "a little more possible."

Others on this side of the island heard dull booms and wondered if the pocket battleship, *Tirpitz*, or some German raider was on the loose.

At the same time, Staff Sergeant David H. Wagner, of the 27th Infantry ("Wolfhound") Regiment, based at Schofield, was leaving his cousin's apartment near Fort Ruger, behind Diamond Head, for St. Andrew's Episcopal Cathedral in Honolulu where he taught Sunday school. As he walked with his cousin toward his car, the owner of the apartment, together with his wife and two children, was standing outside his house, looking in the general direction of Pearl Harbor.

"Isn't it unusual," the latter asked, "to be having AA practice on

Sunday? You can hardly see the planes." Wagner replied that it was unusual but he did not know "anything about it." He continued: "As we drove into the center of the city, I heard an explosion, but thought nothing of it, as blasts were sometimes set off on Sunday, in a quarry in Kaimuki.

"When we arrived at the corner east of the front entrance to the Cathedral Close, we observed that the street was blocked by a crowd of about fifty people, with a policeman standing beyond them, and saying,

" 'Get back, you make a damned good target!'

"I also observed that there was an ambulance in the street in front of the Shumann Carriage Company, across the street from the cathedral, and that the big plate-glass show window of the company was smashed. My instinctive thought was that some crazy man with a gun had smashed the show window, and was shooting up the street.

"It was later reported that a 'Japanese bomb' had landed in the yard of the Governor's Mansion, next to the cathedral chapel, and a fragment of the 'bomb' had killed an old Chinese in front of the Shumann Carriage Company. (It later developed that the 'bomb' was a Navy five-inch AA shell.)

"As the street was blocked, I got out of the car, went around the block and went into the Close from the other (west) side. When I arrived in front of the chapel, I saw that the pre-Sunday school service had already started, and there was a middle-aged man standing outside the chapel, wearing an 'Aloha' shirt. As I came up to him, he said, 'I've come after my children.' When I asked him why, he said, 'Haven't you heard the radio? The Japanese are attacking the island.' "

Meanwhile, the second wave was about to tear at the almost bare bones of Kaneohe Naval Air Station, where all thirty-three planes caught on the ground were burning along with one of their two new hangars. Civilian employees and contractor crews had joined with Navy men in an effort to extinguish the flames and to repair water mains along with electrical lines.

They were still at it when the Japanese swooped in again, strafing and bombing. Blake Clark, a correspondent living in Honolulu reported: "They attacked the contractors' men on their bulldozers. They strafed the men moving the automobiles. They dropped a tremendous bomb on one of the [new] hangars. They shot bullets three-quarters of an inch thick into the hurrying people on the ramp. One of these bullets went through a reinforced concrete wall a foot thick. It left a hole a sewer pipe could have gone through. Wounded people fell, but they did not cry out. A bomb missed a hangar and fell on open ground. The concussion drew a row of riveted steel-sash windows three inches from a wall eighty yards away. Rivets flew from the wall. A hundred yards farther on the concussion knocked down the ordnance man at his gun. Bomb after bomb fell until the administration grounds five hundred yards away were littered with splinters from one to five pounds in weight.

"The ordnance man had his revenge. Coming straight toward him, flying low, just clearing the telephone wires, was a Japanese in a single-seat pursuit plane, strafing after the bombers.

"The ordnance man took less lead this time, pulled his trigger once, and pushed hard against the kicking gun, while it poured its burst of fifty bullets into the Japanese plane.

"Others were undoubtedly shooting at him too. Perhaps it was not the ordnance man who got him. He didn't care. The important thing was that the plane crashed on a knoll of ground near the water. One wheel bounced through a house; the motor landed a quarter of a mile away.

"Another plane was downed in the waters of Kailua Bay. A great cheer went up from the watching crowd, sounding even above the roar of airplanes and machine guns. The rest of the planes flew on toward Ewa."

It was pretty much a Pyrrhic victory. All that Kaneohe could now claim as operational were three PBY's which had been patrolling 120 miles south of Oahu. Heading back, they were still an hour away from home base—and trouble.

At Bellows, ten Japanese planes came in and strafed the aircraft, most of which were obsolete, of the two small squadrons based there. A crash truck and "all possible targets" were soon burning.

Three exceptionally brave pilots, Lieutenants Hans G. Christenson, George Whitman, and Sam Bishop, raced for the few P-40's on the base. Christenson was riddled as he attempted to step into the cockpit.

Whitman gained nearly three hundred feet of altitude when four Zeroes raked his P-40 fore and aft. He crashed into the water. Observers believed he was dead before the flaming fighter splashed into the ocean.

Sam Bishop, his plane also knocked into the surf, was lucky. He struggled out of the canopy he had thrown back just in time and swam ashore.

Perhaps the defenders accounted for one of the attackers. McKinley watched "a stream of white smoke" pouring from an enemy as it "headed out to sea." He couldn't be sure if the weak ground fire from Bellows had scored.

The remaining nine Japanese fighters circled twice and vanished eastward over the water. It was suddenly calm again at the small air base except for the crackling of the flames. A crimson trail led away from the body of the dead pilot. A corpsman beside him, futilely ministering to him, had been hit in the arm, which too was bleeding. But he ignored the wound.

Everyone and everything now was a study in frantic motion. David Wagner forgot his Sunday school class. He started out from Honolulu on the Schofield Barracks bus, which normally had a seated-only rule but was packed with standees.

"As we passed by the east side of Pearl Harbor," he continued, "I observed the *Arizona* sunk and burning, the *Oklahoma* capsized and four others sunk at their moorings. On passing the northeast corner of East Loch, where there was a clear view of the drydock area, I observed the explosion of the destroyer *Shaw*."

Trapped in her floating drydock, the *Shaw* had been hit at 9:30 by a high-level bomber, aiming perhaps at the *Nevada*, passing nearby in her gallant dash for freedom. The destroyer's forward magazine detonated, blowing apart the entire bow. Flames swelled upward. Exploding shells trailed multicolored smoke and streaks of fire flashed and sizzled across the sky in all directions.

This largest blast yet, exceeding even the *Arizona*'s mighty explosion, sank the drydock. It was seen by witnesses for miles around, momentarily blanking out the pillars of smoke from ships, from the oil still burning on the harbor waters and from storage tanks and hangars at Hickam Field.

The concussion apparently was the coup de grâce, as well, for the *Cassin*, already wounded, which rolled over against her drydock mate and sister destroyer, the burning *Downes*. This blast on shore in turn sent the *Downes* off her chocks and into the black, debris-littered waters of the drydock, which had just been flooded in an effort to extinguish the *Downes*' fires.

Ensign Stewart and those remaining on the *Downes* abandoned their guns, jumped and swam to the edge of the dock. His watch might have been safe in Memphis, but as he coughed out the oily, salty slop, he reflected ruefully, "And my four new expensive khakis are still in her. . . ." The uniforms had arrived from the States only two days before.

Even as the *Cassin* settled in against the *Downes*, several overheated warheads aboard the former exploded, causing further carnage to the bow of the *Pennsylvania*, astern. The battleship's forward 5-inch guns had just been put out of commission by a bomb exploding on her boat deck. The three ships could not sink in their dry dock, but they also could not escape the fury of the assault.

The submarine tender *Argonne* herself had been narrowly missed by bombs aimed at the *Nevada*. Aboard her, Yeoman Johnson was now performing messenger duties.

"I remember," he recalled, "there were wounded personnel lying on the dock. The fleet medical officer was attending them. Japanese planes strafed the dock. The doctor then sent his helpers for cover but

U.S.S. Downes and U.S.S. Cassin sunk in drydock. U.S.S. Pennsylvania is in the background.

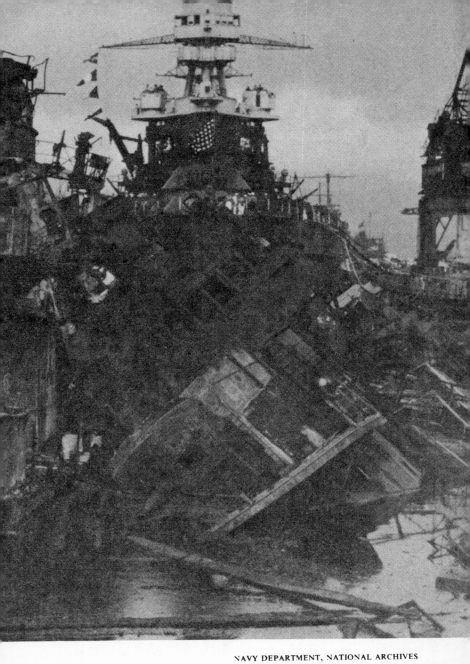

The destroyer Downes burned out and sunk in her drydock.

Ahead of the damaged battleship Pennsylvania in drydock are
the smashed destroyers Cassin and Downes.

Thirty-two crewmen were trapped for thirty-six hours in the capsized hull of the Oklahoma. The Maryland, only slightly damaged, is to the right.

The wrecked Arizona where 1,103
officers and men met their deaths.

A B-17 makes a crash landing at Bellows Field.

Grass grows today on Bellows Field abandoned runway.

continued tending the wounded as though oblivious to what was going on around him.

"He was not wounded, I am quite sure. A .50 caliber from somewhere across the channel fired through the side of the *Argonne* wounded a man in the laundry."

About the time of the *Shaw*'s explosion, the *Nevada* was steered to an anchorage off Hospital Point. Signal hoists from shore had ordered Lieutenant Commander Francis Thomas, the senior officer on board, to keep out of the channel, in other words, to discontinue the battleship's bid for the open sea.

Lower and lower in the water she sank, and it looked as though the attackers would succeed in blocking the channel with the great bulk of the twenty-six-year-old *Nevada,* the oldest battleship present. Had this happened, it might have required weeks to clear an adequate passage.

The *California*, carrying the flag of Vice Admiral William S. Pye, Annapolis class of 1901, commanding Battle Force, had been torpedoed and bombed until it was touch-and-go whether she would capsize, as had the *Oklahoma* and the *Utah*. Counter-flooding, ordered by Lieutenant Commander Marion N. Little, the first lieutenant, kept her on even keel, although she was slowly sinking. In spite of her difficulties, some of her guns continued to blast away through the smoke.

"A whole stick of bombs," Little would report, "landed on our starboard side in the water between the ship and the shore. A few seconds later, the ship was hit by a bomb amidships on the starboard side. There was a heavy explosion below decks followed by light smoke from the starboard side and later heavy smoke.

"This bombing was followed by strafing with machine guns. Such guns of our battery as had ammunition and could bear were in action. I informed central of the bomb hit amidships and ordered Repair Party One to report to the scene. There appeared to be several recurrent waves of strafing attacks but no further bombing.

"I returned to the captain [Captain J.W. Bunkley, now back from swimming at Waikiki where he had been when the attack commenced], who was on the emergency platform and gave him a brief summary of the damage at that time insofar as I knew it. From there I went to the quarterdeck intending to enter the main deck and reach the scene of the fire which was then raging on the starboard side in the interior of the ship. I undogged the door on the starboard side of the quarterdeck leading into the main deck but was met by a rush of heavy smoke and heat so intense that it was impossible to enter the compartment.

"I closed the door and started to enter the crew's reception room, hoping to get in that way but found the same conditions existing there.

I started across to the port side, intending to get inside to the main deck, but upon my arrival noted that the fire on the next ship astern [the *Maryland*] had worked down to the oil which formed a heavy coating on the surface of the water and was coming down rapidly toward the *California* with the wind, which was blowing a fresh breeze from that direction."

Captain Bunkley, now joined by Admiral Pye, decided to abandon ship.

Commander Little "slid down one of the lines to the quay where I remained temporarily. Fire passed down the port side, setting many fires on the weather decks, but the ship as a whole did not catch fire.

"Seeing that the fire was passing I swam over from the quay to the dredge pontoons and went inshore to where a large group of men were gathered at the water's edge and ordered them to return to the ship in an attempt to salvage her. I myself returned to the quay in a punt and climbed up the mooring lines to the deck where I started to organize the personnel to fight the fires still burning amidships and to prevent the ship from sinking or capsizing."

Thus, the *California* was a unique case of a capital ship being abandoned and remanned all within the space of a few minutes, thanks partly to a windshift.

The "don't give up the ship" spirit was manifested throughout Pearl Harbor. Men who had been blown overboard by explosions, who had slipped off the slimy decks and been rescued or who had gone ashore for some purpose kept coming back to their infernos in an attempt to save them. All sorts of launches, workboats, tugs and such unglamorous harbor craft as water tenders and even one "honey barge" or garbage scow came to their aid.

Commander Hobby of the *Oklahoma* continued, "I saw the *Oklahoma* officers and men who boarded the *Maryland* go to the *Maryland* antiaircraft battery and aid in the firing."

Hobby, certain that others were clear of the upturned hull, stripped down and was about to dive, "expecting to swim in," when he was picked up by a motor launch which then cruised up and down, hauling survivors out of the oily water.

On a dock he noticed a gathering cluster of Navy men "asking where they could go to aid in antiaircraft fire; all seemed to be thinking of how to fight rather than seeking safety." Some of the *Oklahoma*'s displaced personnel were already aboard the tanker *Neosho*, passing ammunition.

The minelayer *Oglala*'s crew was also forced to abandon her. Shortly before 10:00, she became the third ship to capsize. Admiral Furlong himself slid gracefully down the old Fall River Liner's high starboard side to join the mounting number of officers and enlisted men who no longer possessed a ship they could call their own.

Off the west coast, Lieutenant Welch chased yet another enemy plane seaward and caught it, some five miles off Barber's Point. Between them, Welch and Taylor downed seven planes that morning. The latter was already grounded because of his bleeding leg.

Turning back, Welch looked about the skies, shielding his eyes against the dazzling morning sun. He saw only black smoke columns still boiling up from Pearl Harbor and Hickam Field, but "no Japs!" There were none. It was 10:00 A.M. The attack was over.

CHAPTER 8

The last drone of the final attacking plane had faded off across the Pacific. The *Enterprise* and *Lexington* had already launched their airplanes in search of what certainly must have been phantom Japanese carriers. They flew off toward the west and south sectors primarily, instead of to the northwest where the task force now was turning, victoriously, homeward.

Expecting another eruption from the skies, soldiers, sailors and civilians worked at a fevered pace with what little materials were available. At Shafter, Harold Cook began to string the barbed wire which he had trucked down from Schofield, at great peril. "Though the attack was short in duration," he observed, "it seemed like eternity." He had hardly unrolled his first length of the tough, prickly barricade when he and others were ordered down to Waikiki: "We heard that Japanese paratroopers had landed on the island."

Even the otherwise laconic and hardheaded duty watch logs at the stations and bases on Oahu bore testament to parachutists "landing" at widely dispersed locations, from Barber's Point to Kahuku. One Navy notation described the mythical invaders as garbed in "blue coveralls, red emblems."

Bellows, utilizing all available soldiers and precious guns, herded the field's families into one building. Then, when it was discovered that the rifles were all empty, the lieutenant in command raced off to the ordnance depot. Returning with a few rounds of .30-caliber ammunition, he then sent a corporal off to find some cots, if possible, so that shelters could be established inside a storage tunnel under one of the flanking hills.

Other troops were ordered to move as fast as they could down a secondary base road "because of rumored snipers."

Corporal McKinley's men "were called together and organized into a defense set-up. They expected invasion; they prepared gun positions on the beach and manned them. They dug pits, set machine guns up and by this time had the canvas machine gun belts loaded: canvas strap with slots—the clips did not work correctly. The casual detail positions: four .30-caliber machine guns and two .50-caliber."

At 10:30, all civilian doctors available were called to Tripler Army Hospital. Within the next hour, martial law was declared.

It wasn't a moment too soon. Many stores had been damaged or set on fire by antiaircraft shells. Looting was a real possibility.

Military families were trying as best they could to meet and cope with their wholly unheralded new way of life. Mrs. Ostenberg, at Wheeler, was given an early noon meal at headquarters "along with the troops."

She continued: "At the dinner table, the officers discussed the attack and the warning given by a private of the Signal Corps who had picked up the planes coming in while he was working on a newly installed, improved radar set which had just been received from the States.

"Later in the afternoon we were bussed back to our house to pack a suitcase and be ready to move, as all dependents were to be taken into Honolulu that night, the idea being, that if an invasion came, Honolulu would be declared an open city and there would be no fighting there."

At Pearl Harbor chaos reigned almost to the extent it had during the attack. Fires still burned fiercely, as crews struggled to save those ships that were not already sunk or destroyed.

The *Raleigh* remained afloat through the Herculean efforts of her crew, jettisoning everything from torpedo tubes to life rafts, shifting ballast constantly and even stuffing lifebelts in the bomb holds. But she was afire and in bad shape, having been pounced upon again and again because she, like the *Utah*, had occupied a carrier berth.

Nonetheless, the cruiser still was able to send a carpenter with cutting tools over to the neighboring bulk of the capsized target battleship. Machinist S.A. Szymanski and others who had abandoned the *Utah* were seeking cover on adjacent Ford Island when they thought they heard "knockings" from the hull.

Aided by others, Szymanski was able to get through the steel plates in a remarkably few minutes and hauled to safety John B. Vaessen, a fireman, who had survived relatively unharmed in an airspace under a dynamo room.

Thus the fifty-nine figured as "lost" on the old battleship now were reduced by one.

Dr. Niiranen, the dentist attached to the *Utah*, began the necessary task of identifying the badly burned dead through dental work.

At 3:00 P.M., Admiral Kimmel received General Marshall's warning telegram: 'Just what significance the hour set may have, we do not know, but be on the alert accordingly . . . ." The Japanese messenger who had been sent to deliver it had been stopped countless times en route to Shafter. Guards thought his uniform resembled that of a paratrooper, although it was wholly unlikely that any MP or Honolulu policeman had even seen a real-life Japanese paratrooper.

Overshadowed by the day's holocaust was the attack on two private planes, from John Rogers Field, east of Hickam. By a quirk of fate, both fliers and passengers made it down, but a civilian pilot on the field, Robert Tyce, was killed by strafing.

And so a midwinter's afternoon moved on into evening. Oahu became a symphony of sounds—the click and scoop of spades as shallow trench shelters were being dug in parks and school grounds, the scrape of bulldozers clearing away rubble, and the far more strident, metallic noise at the naval base as all available repair and rescue crews ripped away hunks of ships' sides and bored into hardened armor plate, still searching for those who might be alive.

But there just wasn't enough salvage equipment for disaster of such avalanche proportions.

Lights were shaded or dispensed with altogether. How soon would the foe wing back to greater vengeance? Voices were muted.

Mrs. Ostenberg's husband saw her and their children off to the bus "that was to take us into the city. It was raining and dark and I was carrying the younger child and a suitcase. We boarded the crowded buses and started on that terrible five-hour trip from Wheeler Field to Honolulu.

"We drove through all kinds of firing, as our antiaircraft was at work and shells were bursting all around us. There were no lights on the buses in our convoy, but fires from Ford Island and Pearl Harbor lit up the road. There seemed to be fires everywhere and the rain was not enough to put them out.

"It was most hectic in that schoolhouse with no lights where we were taken. Everyone had brought their pets and there was never a quiet moment all through the night. Either a baby was crying, or a dog barking, and occasionally the drone of a plane engine overhead. We all lived in fear of another attack, or an invasion."

Other residents ate early, at 5:00 or 5:30 P.M., in their strangely blacked-out kitchens. Probably not one person in a hundred doubted that the invaders would return before, or certainly by, morning.

It was, as Corporal McKinley at Bellows observed, "a period of great nervous tension and excitement. There were many false alarms and much haphazard shooting. The men stayed in their machine gun pits, too frightened to sleep. The common Portuguese man-of-war, floating in the water near the beach, reflecting the moon light, resulted in much shooting. One soldier thought he saw a landing craft coming in to shore in the area below Waimanalo Beach. Bellows Field men took trucks, light weapons, started out, then received the report that it was a false alarm."

The duty log at Bellows laconically spoke of the night's confusion.

0300—Message read re friendly surface craft coming into Pearl Harbor.

0305—Home Guard report arrest of Jap family flashing lights. Detail sent for them.

0320—Jap boy from above brought in. Claims father ill (seemed to have fever). Boy taken to nurse for verification of story re father.

0330—Story partly verified. Boy held, family and house watched.

0330—Report of green flare from beach by beach guard—detail sent out to investigate.

0540—7 P-40's in—got lost in clouds and got over Pearl Harbor when AA opened up they came home. No enemy activity.

0707—Ground Defense Officer accepted Jap sailor who swam ashore (first POW—officer of midget sub.)

The officer was Ensign Kazuo Sakamaki, who unsuccessfully had attempted to scuttle his small undersea craft. His shipmate drowned. The surrender was a small victory in a day of abject defeat, something for which Americans were emotionally unprepared.

To all who knew and loved Hawaii as well as the services and service people stationed there it was as though there had been many deaths in one close family.

And yet, the rising activity from Kahuku Point to Waikiki, from Kaneohe Bay to Makaha was scarcely a dirge. The sounds seemed to whisper of the rebirth of an island and its people who refused to die.

CHAPTER 9

On Monday morning, December 8, President Roosevelt stood before a joint session of Congress and asked for a declaration of war against Japan. He observed, "Yesterday, December 7th, a day which will live in infamy, the United States of America was suddenly and deliberately attacked by naval and air forces of the Empire of Japan. . . ."

The Senate's vote in support of the resolution was unanimous. In the House the vote was 388-1; the lone dissenter was Congresswoman Jeannette Rankin, a Republican from Montana, who had also voted against a war with the Kaiser's Germany in 1917. She cried as she registered her "no."

As the President spoke, Hawaii began to dig itself out from the disaster. There were two immediate priorities: first, to rescue the wounded and the dying from the wrecked battleships and the destroyed airfields, and to care for them along with the civilian casualties in Honolulu; the second, to prepare the populace for the possibility of invasion.

Security agents immediately began picking up enemy aliens. By Monday they had taken into custody 482 persons: 370 Japanese, 98 Germans and 14 Italians. This did not constitute the entire enemy alien population of Hawaii. There were several hundred more, including the aged and infirm, who were not considered dangerous.

The Major Disaster Council, just six months old, was the first civilian volunteer agency to swing into action. Governor Joseph Poindexter designated this as the Office of Civilian Defense.

One of OCD's first moves was to marshal its volunteers, who turned out with civilian trucks and drivers, many coming in from the plantations. These trucks were hurriedly fitted with litters and dispatched to docks and air bases to supplement the military transports, bringing in the wounded. They also carried additional medical supplies to aid field doctors who were treating the wounded on the spot.

Many Honolulu surgeons had assembled Sunday in a local auditorium to hear an address by Dr. John J. Moorhead on the techniques of wound surgery. The address was never delivered. The audience had to learn for themselves—first-hand.

Most of the naval casualties were taken to the Pearl Harbor Naval Hospital or treated on the hospital ship *Solace*. Other hospitals on the island of Oahu took their full quota, but there were too many patients and not enough equipment for the enormous task involved.

By December 8, doctors had run out of operating gowns and were effecting surgery in pajamas or their underwear. There was blood everywhere. When surgeons ran out of surgical masks, they used torn sheets, but when they exhausted the supply of rubber gloves, there were no substitutes. So many doctors were on duty they had to share surgical instruments, passing them from table to table.

The Hawaiian blood bank contained a mere two hundred units of plasma, all of which had been exhausted in the first six hours after the attack. As the result of radio and newspaper pleas, donors came forward from all over the island to provide the urgently needed blood.

The Navy suffered the heaviest losses—2,036 killed, most of them in the first ten minutes of action. The Marines lost 109 officers and men. An additional eight hundred men, belonging to the two sister services, were wounded. Nearly half of the Navy and Marine casualties were aboard the *Arizona*. The Army sustained 218 deaths and 364 wounded. There were sixty-eight civilians dead and thirty-five wounded, although there may be slight discrepancies in these latter figures. Eighteen ships were sunk or badly damaged, 188 planes, about evenly divided between Army and Navy, were destroyed, and 160 more were damaged.

The price for this annihilation—3,630 dead and wounded—was absurdly cheap. The Japanese lost twenty-nine planes, one large and five midget submarines, fifty-five air crewmen, and possibly as many as sixty or seventy Imperial Navy personnel. Of these, nine were aboard the "vest pocket" submersibles.

As the War Department would note: "The Japanese caught the United States Army about three months short of completing what had been planned as the most intensive phase of its rearmament." It was a pitiful understatement.

Coupled with simultaneous strikes on the Philippines, which also knocked out United States' airpower, and on the main British squadron off Singapore, sinking the battleship *Prince of Wales* and the battle cruiser *Repulse*, Japan's dash along the high road to victory seemed assured. "Rarely," wrote the historian Walter Millis, "has there been so brilliant a success in the history of warfare."

If there was any comfort at all to be nursed out of the debacle, it lay in the conduct of those under attack. Commanding officers recorded hundreds of acts of heroism in keeping with the highest tradition of the naval service. Rear Admiral Thomas B. Inglis, then Chief of Naval Intelligence, would testify, "No instance is recorded in which the behavior of crews or individuals left anything to be desired." As a testament to his statement, fifteen Medals of Honor and sixty Navy Crosses were awarded by the Navy, and five Distinguished Service Crosses and sixty-five Silver Stars by the Army.

From the United States' perspective, everything had gone wrong, from Washington to Honolulu. Medical supplies were scarce. Anesthesia narcotics, for example, had been locked in vaults, complying with federal law, and could not be obtained until Monday.

The hastily ordered blackout had resulted in monumental traffic snarls and many accidents. Police Chief W.A. Gabrielsen's first radio message to the people was to "stay calm and stay home." Then the police and the fire department asked for volunteers and were so swamped with men answering the call they could not utilize all the untrained hands.

The police also suddenly realized they didn't have enough guns or ammunition for the volunteers. They appealed to the Army, which was not a great deal better off, for armament to help patrolmen guard piers and utilities.

Meanwhile, the OCD had placed guards at every crossroad and bridge. Unfortunately, they were armed only with clubs, knives used for cutting sugar cane, and obsolete guns. By midnight of December 8, there were 3,800 volunteers on duty on Oahu and thousands of others on the other islands. There was fear that public utilities would be sabotaged. Navy Commander Wilmer Thompson, assigned to the Public Works Department, joined fellow employees to "sleep at night on our metal top desks. We did the best we could, despite those waves of dive-bombing mosquitoes swept in by the Kona winds."

Commander Thompson was ordered to design camouflage paint schemes for several water towers on the base in the hopes they could not be seen by attacking planes. However, he "never could understand why any human mentality could think that a building could be hidden by painting it." He thought blackout enforcement was often equally ludicrous. One evening, "listening to Tokyo Rose on the radio . . . there came an angry knock on the door." Light was showing—through the keyhole!

The University of Hawaii ROTC was called to service and, including high school ROTC units, the Territorial Guard numbered 35 officers and 370 men. The American Legion was summoned by radio and within one hour some four hundred veterans from World

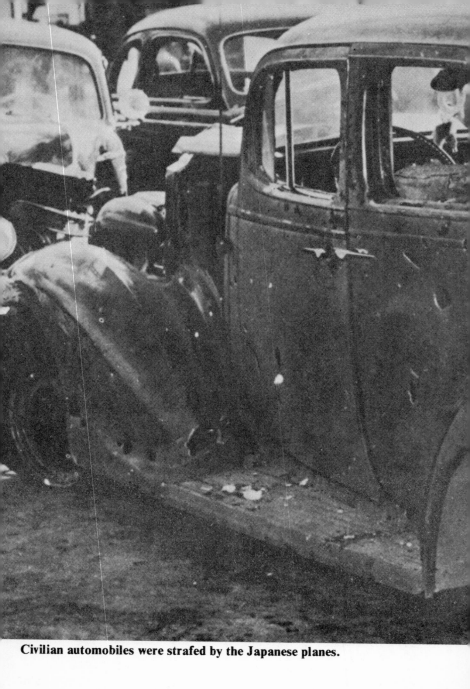
Civilian automobiles were strafed by the Japanese planes.

Civilian defense workers attempting to extinguish burning building.

War I had reported for duty, as well as men who had fought in 1898, now in their sixties and seventies.

The youngest members of the Hawaiian community, the Boy Scouts and Girl Scouts, were among the most useful. On many of the islands, they were one of the few organized groups that could be easily contacted. Moreover, with their bicycles and motor bikes, they were mobile.

The Boy Scouts aided the police in many ways. To relieve the overloaded telephone system, they were sent from plantation to plantation to warn the rural citizens of the tight new blackout regulations. They carried buckets of black paint, so that the headlights of rural automobiles could be shielded, except for a narrow slit. The older Boy Scouts were taught to direct traffic, allowing the police to turn their attention toward sabotage, enemy aliens, and with the F.B.I. and the Army, preparations for an "invasion." On Molokai, the Boy Scouts patrolled the streets for four months until the armed forces took over. They were also used with rescue squads, to carry the wounded to litters, and in fire-fighting operations.

Even the smallest Girl Scouts worked full days, cooking, washing dishes, scrubbing, and minding hundreds of children evacuated from the air bases and civilian homes.

Between five and six thousand women, children, aged, infirm and other evacuees were brought through the blacked-out night of December 7 and 8 from the air bases and off-base quarters to Honolulu.

When this evacuation was completed, the Major Disaster Council had on its hands what constituted a whole town of refugees who had to be fed and housed for an indefinite period of time. The University of Hawaii and many school buildings were used as refugee centers. Canteens and soup lines were set up. Eventually, Navy ship stores were opened so that evacuees who were housed with private citizens could get food.

The business community of Honolulu was of enormous help. Merchants opened their stores and provided blankets, flashlights, candles, material for blackouts and emergency equipment.

Food became an item of concern. Decisions on a system of rationing had to be made. Thousands of volunteer workers had to be fed while doing their jobs.

Governor Poindexter had spoken with President Roosevelt on December 7 and elicited a promise of ships with food. But in the meantime, grocery stores were ordered to close for one day in order to take inventory. On December 9, all liquor sales were banned. Three Japanese banks were closed.

Unfortunately, the volunteer workers did not have uninterrupted access to restaurants, which were ordered to close at 5:00 P.M. in observance of the blackout. Therefore, the Red Cross and the Salvation Army set up canteens to provide thousands of guards, policemen and other workers with food and drink.

A great deal of the damage had been caused by American antiaircraft shells which fell back in the area immediately north of Waikiki Beach. The missiles had been fired from active batteries of Fort de Russey. The Chinese stores along McCully Street, near the Ala Wai Canal, had been burned. A drugstore was among the total losses. The owner, his wife and two girls, who lived above, perished.

In all, about a half million dollars' worth of civilian property was damaged or destroyed.

Meanwhile, the Navy continued its search for men who might still be living within air bubbles deep inside the *Oklahoma, Utah* and *Arizona*. However, there was not much hope except in the case of the *Oklahoma*, where tappings continued to echo from her upturned keel.

At first, the rescue teams, led by Julio de Castro, a civilian at the Navy Yard, employed acetylene torches. The naked flame, however, threatened to set pockets of oil afire and asphyxiate those imprisoned. There was also the danger of explosion. Compressed air hammer and mechanical cutters proved safer and almost as effective as the standard burning process.

On Monday, twenty-four hours after the bombing, six men, grimy but smiling, emerged from a newly cut, jagged opening. Three hours later, at 11:00 A.M. eleven more were found and dragged to safety from the *Oklahoma*. At 2:00 P.M., another five were rescued and at 4:00, eight more emerged into the bright sunshine. Despite lack of sleep, food and sufficient oxygen, the survivors were judged to be in "good shape."

But this as not the finale. At 2:00 A.M. Tuesday, the last of the thirty-two survivors were hauled out of their black, watery prison. They were Second Class Machinist Mates J.P. Centers and W.F. Staff. The latter would write: "About Monday noon we heard tapping and we answered them. After so long they were right overhead and we could hear them talking. When they started to cut into us, it let out air and we were under air pressure, the water came up as our air escaped.

"The water ran out the hole they were cutting and they left. But we still had about six inches of air space. . . . we started tapping again. The rescuers got . . . to us again."

After remaining sixty hours without respite atop the hull of the *Oklahoma*, Commander Hobby left the ship. It was all over. He had done his best to cheat the heavy death toll. In this disaster, second only to that of the *Arizona*, 415 perished out of a ship's complement of 1354.

Others lived, despite their entombment, for longer periods. When the *West Virginia*, on which 105 died, was raised in May, 1942, it was found that three men had survived in a pump room until December 23, sixteen long hopeless days after the attack. Final scribbled notes attested to the ordeal.

Everywhere around Pearl Harbor there persisted morbid canvas of death and destruction. When the *Lexington* arrived later in the week, an officer coming aboard with dispatches exclaimed: "Gosh, it's great to see something afloat!"

While the rescue and salvage operations were proceeding, echoes of war were being felt in an unusual epilogue upon Niihau, the most westerly and most isolated island of the principal Hawaiian group. Nothing was heard of the bombings until about 2:00 P.M. that Sunday when a Japanese plane crashed in a field near the home of Hawila Kaleohano. Even though Kaleohano didn't realize the United States had been attacked by Japan, he saw that the plane was riddled with bullets. He disarmed the pilot and put him under guard until he could get help from Kauai.

As interpreters he used Yoshito Harada, an American citizen, and Ishimatsu Shintani. Having admitted that Oahu had been attacked, the pilot sent Shintani back to Kaleohano with a bribe of $200 for the release of his papers.

In the meantime, the pilot persuaded Harada to help him pull the machine guns off the plane. The two then so terrorized the villagers that they took refuge in nearby caves.

The following Friday, Kaleohano and four other men escaped from Niihau and rowed to Kauai, sixteen hours away, for help. But on Saturday morning, the two "outlaw" Japanese captured Benehakaka Kanahele and his wife, to be held as hostages. When the pilot turned his back, Kanahele managed to grab him by the neck and dashed his head against a stone wall, killing him. Seeing that he was no longer protected, Harada turned his gun on himself.

Kaleohano returned early Sunday morning with an American Army lieutenant of Japanese ancestry and thirteen enlisted men, only to find that the "Battle of Niihau" was over.

In the initial weeks after the attack, tension mounted and in addition to the fear of invasion, Hawaii began to anticipate all manner of sabotage. There were rumors that the reservoirs had been poisoned. The police told the public to boil water.

The Office of Civilian Defense continued to receive reports of parachutists. There were tales that the Japanese plantation workers had defected and fired on American soldiers; a story about a milk truck that had opened machine gun fire on Hickam Field; a rumor that there was a renegade radio station operating to jam legitimate

American messages; and reports that fires were deliberately being set in cane fields or lights left on to signal enemy planes coming in on one sabotage mission or another. A Shinto priest was fined $400 and sentenced to one year at hard labor for keeping the eternal altar flame burning despite blackout. He was later paroled.

The *Advertiser* ran a story that the security agents were taking more Japanese aliens into custody "for their own protection."

The Japanese quarter of Honolulu had been most heavily damaged and of those killed in the December 7 attack, 80 per cent were of Japanese ancestry. The newspaper ran lists of the unidentified dead in the morgue, such as "No name, Japanese male, unidentified" or "No name, Oriental baby, female, eight months." For a Caucasian, "No name, age thirty-five, male, no address, dead on arrival, had initials H.A.D. on shirt . . . in morgue."

Yet life somehow went on. By December 18, the *Advertiser* carried a front page story: "War is no bar to marriage nor obstacle to true love. . . . More than one hundred applications were filed with the Honolulu agent during the first three days (of this week) Monday through Wednesday."

After days of nothing but war news, and much of that censored, the newspaper returned the society page to its editions. First among the items reported was that Miss Dorothy Plooey had been married on December 14 to Sergeant Thomas Delbridge at Hickam Field. This same day's paper carried a large picture of Niihau's hero, Kanahele, recuperating from his wounds in the hospital.

And babies were still being born: a son to Mrs. Harold Bloomfield on December 21. The boy's great-great-grandfather had been Samuel Dwight, a member of the twelfth shipload of missionaries to arrive in Hawaii.

Perhaps oddest of all was the occasional obituary. After December 7, it seemed strange to be reminded that people could die of natural causes.

On December 22, a commission arrived from Washington, headed by Associate Justice Owen J. Roberts, whose task it was to investigate the Pearl Harbor disaster.

In the meantime, the Navy was taking a hard second look at the injury done to its ships. Among the battleships, hopes were entertained for the *Pennsylvania*, the *Maryland* and the *Tennessee*—hopes that, with a lot of hard work, paid off.

The *Pennsylvania* had not been badly damaged. She had lost one of her 5-inch .51-caliber guns to a Japanese bomb which had exploded two decks below. This gun was replaced by a similar gun from the flooded *West Virginia*. Her ruptured water mains and electrical circuits were repaired, and all other explosion damage, including that which had ruptured her steel structure, was repaired in drydock. By December 20, the *Pennsylvania* was ready to leave the Navy Yard.

By the same date, the *Maryland* had been made seaworthy. Since one of the two bombs which hit the ship exploded at water level, inside the ship, there was flooding. Her bow drooped downward about five feet. Moreover, on the port side, another bomb had torn a hole in the *Maryland* about twelve feet by twenty feet. To save the drydocks for ships with greater problems, the Navy Yard, with the help of the *Maryland*'s crew, repaired her afloat. If ordered, she could have gone into action against the Japanese before New Year's.

For a ship that was not so seriously hit, the *Tennessee* was in the worst position of all, for she was so firmly wedged between the quay on her inboard side and the sunken *West Virginia* on her outboard that even when full steam was applied to her engines, she didn't budge. The *Tennessee* was lightened by pumping a half million gallons of fuel from her bunkers. On December 20, she was ready to steam away from what had almost been her grave.

The *Helena*, one of three torpedoed cruisers whose gunners were credited with shooting down several Japanese planes, sailed the same week for the Mare Island Navy Yard, San Francisco.

Christmas Day came to the Islands . . . solemnly.

On that morning, Admiral Chester W. Nimitz, the trim fifty-six-year-old former submariner, arrived in Pearl Harbor by flying boat. The new Commander in Chief of the Pacific Fleet, wearing civvies, looked about him and observed: "This is a terrible sight!" A barge of oil-soaked corpses had just passed by his launch. Recovery was still continuing.

When he arrived in fleet headquarters, the soft-spoken admiral announced to the duty officer, "My name is Nimitz." As if the subordinate didn't know! Then, as Admiral Kimmel walked forward, his successor shook hands and murmured, "It might have happened to me." It probably came far too late to help the morale of Kimmel, who was being pressured by the White House to retire. The equally unlucky General Short had already been relieved by Lieutenant General Delos C. Emmons.

It was an especially sad December 25 for families such as Major Ostenberg's. Many of them sailed for the mainland that day aboard the *Mariposa*.

Christmas week was, necessarily, a darkened one. Nor were there many trees, which were normally shipped in from the west coast. All large holiday functions had been cancelled. After the mass burials on Oahu, who had the heart?

Then as a New Year's eve salute, enemy submarines shelled the islands of Hawaii and Kauai. Piers were hit at Hilo, on the "big island," and a gasoline tank at Nawiliwili, Kauai. Two weeks previously, a pineapple cannery on Maui had been slightly damaged by a brief shelling. But on none of the three islands had there been any casualties.

And so, 1942 was ushered in. Hawaii was blacked out. All guns were manned.

CHAPTER 10

Hawaii went to war with spirit and resolve. Her role was reminiscent of England in the first weeks of conflict.

As the soldiers and pilots had discovered on December 7, there really was not much "hardware" available with which to repel a determined assault. The Navy, while equipped with many of her "heavies" that Sunday morning, had not been ready to use them.

As one subterfuge, the Army sent out a hurry-up call for all available carpenters and put them to work building dummy plywood airplanes and dispersed them about open fields. But there was no purpose in arming the home guard with fake guns. These would not, at close range, fool the blindest of saboteurs.

Personal revolvers, pistols, rifles and shotguns, antique or not, were now in demand as first-line weaponry. Filipino-Hawaiians still trusted their sugar cane knives, which they could wield with murderous accuracy.

During those first months of war, supply ships were relatively few and far between. Most of the Merchant Marine had been and still were in the Atlantic, playing a not too successful game of hide-and-seek with the U-boats.

General MacArthur expressed the frustration of Allied commanders in the Pacific when he observed that it was "incredible . . . no effort was made to bring in supplies." Added to their frustration was the not unfounded suspicion that priority was being accorded the war in Europe.

Hawaiians themselves were too busy, for the most part, to complain. There was much to be done and challenges aplenty for everyone, young and old.

The educational system was especially hard hit. After December 7, schools were shut down. Those which opened did so with staffs reduced by one-fourth or more. Teachers were off to war, in or out of uniform. Twenty-nine schools were turned into hospitals or offices for various emergency organizations. In those institutions where the familiar class bells did sound as before, some of the gymnasiums, cafeterias or chemistry laboratories were temporary homes to draft boards, rationing councils and the like.

"I remember," Charlotte Frances, of Washington, D.C., then twelve, would recall, "when we came back to school we were issued gas masks and taught to jump into the trenches which had been dug around the school.

"But I remember best the great enormous barrels which were filled with water and placed at intervals on the various floors. If the Japanese attacked us with mustard gas, we were to tear off our clothes and jump in. I remember that as time went on, I was disappointed because the opportunity never came."

Hawaiians' pride in their colorful past was immediately evident when the cultural committee entrusted with safe-guarding Hawaiian art treasures tried to remove the honored statue of King Kamehameha I from its prominent position in front of the Iolani Palace on King Street. The islanders put up a tremendous storm of protest. Kamehameha, the Great Warrior who had led the Hawaiians with spirit and determination, was regarded as a sign of unity and victory. The cultural committee retreated before the hue and cry. And the bronze Kamehameha remained where he was on his tall pedestal for all to see.

So while the paintings and rare collections, the chandeliers and fine porcelains were carefully wrapped and stowed away, the Army was placing more and more responsibility on the willing and capable shoulders of the Hawaiian people.

In early 1942, many more organizations, which had no particular parallel with war-time groups in the United States, were formed. There was the Organized Defense Volunteers, whose job was to help in repelling invaders. They numbered 20,000 men. There was another called the Hawaii Defense Volunteers, composed mainly of Chinese-Hawaiians, but with some Koreans, Hawaiians and Filipinos. The Women's Air Raid Defense (WARDS), a group of young Honolulu society women who started training with the Army on New Year's Day a few months later, became a part of the Army's air alert system. The Businessmen's Military Training Corps was organized primarily to deal with enemy aliens in time of invasion. They maintained files on the location of all aliens on the Islands.

The Boy Scouts on Oahu seized the opportunity, when they were reorganized with Boy Scouts in Hawaii, to change their name to the Oahu Volunteer Infantry.

The 120,000 Japanese-Hawaiians were left out. At first, realizing their peculiar position, they seemed reluctant to volunteer and were therefore suspect. At the same time, with rumors of sabotage continuing, local and military authorities almost automatically excluded them from police or guard duty, any work in "restricted" or "confidential" areas, essential industrial tasks, censorship, air raid defense and related activities.

Well over four-fifths of the children of Japanese ancestry in Hawaii attended Japanese language schools in addition to their regular schooling. Many were later sent back to Japan for higher education. An estimated 100,000 Buddhists worshipped in Hawaii on December 7 and at least 50,000 at Shinto shrines.

Japan recognized dual citizenship and still thought of these naturalized Americans as Japanese. Their theory was popularly called "law of the blood" and was in direct contradiction to United States law, which did not recognize duality, favoring instead "law of the soil."

By the spring of 1942, prejudice against the Japanese began to dissipate. The young Japanese-Americans who had been summarily dismissed from the Territorial Guards after Pearl Harbor were formed into a labor battalion attached to the Army Engineers at Schofield Barracks.

The first mainland troops in any quantity began to arrive in Hawaii in April and kept coming until, by June, there were 135,000 as compared with 43,000 on December 7.

Tent bivouacs dotted the plains from Schofield Barracks to the north and east coasts. Not only was Hawaii an excellent staging ground, transit area and nerve center of command, but its terrain simulated some of that to be found in those Pacific islands tagged for subsequent invasion.

Small arms and the concussion from heavier "stuff" echoed off the volcanic heights of Oahu, Hawaii and other islands. Men charged up the steep, scrubby ridges, with whoops reminiscent of Gettysburg and San Juan Hill. Soldiers developed a fierce pride in their outfits, fashioning spontaneous signs such as: "Danger Ahead! Infantry Dug In!" followed by their unit numbers.

Salvage operations remained a top priority. Equipment shipped to Hawaii for this purpose included lumber shorings, pumps, torches and steel cables for winches to be employed in righting capsized ships. All, however, continued in short supply.

It was a slimy, muddy, perilous job and the demand for specialized labor exceeded anything the Hawaiian market itself could supply. Soon, groups of women in water-resistant white coveralls were taking their places beside experienced men on the grimy, barnacled outjuttings of the wrecked ships. Trained on-the-job as acetylene torch cutters to slice away the twisted sections which obstructed pumping and raising, they proved a valuable supplement to the experts flown in from the mainland.

In charge of this giant "push" was Captain Homer N. Wallin, of Seattle, who as a young ensign (Annapolis Class of '17) had been assigned to the Navy's Construction Corps. At the time of Pearl Harbor, he was Senior Battle Force Engineer in Hawaii. This energetic specialist knew the complicated insides of many of the sunken vessels as well as some doctors know their patients.

During the complex operation, four men were killed. Two were overcome by hydrogen sulphide gas while working on the *Nevada* and two died in the watery maze of the *Arizona,* after their acetylene torches ignited gases.

The *Shaw,* which had exploded so spectacularly, received a new bow graft and was sent off to Mare Island, San Francisco, under her own power. The *West Virginia* was raised in May. The Navy Yard also worked on the destroyers *Cassin* and *Downes,* both so wrecked that their hulls had to be rebuilt, although most of the machinery had come through intact. In combat with the Japanese, the *Cassin* would win seven battle stars and the *Downes,* four.

The two other mammoth undertakings of that spring were the floating of the *Nevada* and the *California.*

With the addition of salvage workers and military personnel, and in the face of inadequate shipping in waters alive with enemy submarines, food became one of Hawaii's most critical problems. In order to protect Hawaii in case of emergency, Congress appropriated $35 million for food stocks, mostly staples, to be shipped to the Islands as reserves.

Among the imports from the United States came 2,500 cases of empty Coca-Cola bottles to Honolulu and such strange items as a full year's supply of sardines, the Pacific parallel of "Coals to Newcastle."

Most of the truck farmers in the Islands were alien Japanese. During the months after December 7, these people thought they would be deported or interned. Therefore, they hesitated to plant or harvest.

Unfortunately, the summer of 1942 was marked by a ruinous drought which parched the hastily planted crops. The drought was so severe that, on Oahu, the only vegetable which came up was the lima bean. So they ate lima beans—and carrots, the only vegetable which came in from the States. Commenting on the "Remember Pearl Harbor" slogan, which had already been coined, the Hawaii *Star-Bulletin* wrote: ". . . the Island housewife . . . is often heard to say 'remember . . . celery?' "

With the lack of interisland communications, each island faced its own particular problem. For example, Molokai grew no lima beans or

Damage to property in Honolulu.

Damage to property in Honolulu was estimated at more than half a million dollars.

**Much of it, however, was caused
by anti aircraft fire going awry.**

US ARMY PHOTOS

**Wheeler Field was badly hit by a wave of planes
streaking down through Kole-Kole Pass.**

heeler Air Force Base today doubles as a bedding
ea for service families and a link in the Air Force's
mmuications and electronics complex in the Pacific.

Pumehana Street, Honolulu, on December 7, 1941.

US ARMY PHOTO

And as it looks today.

ARMY TIMES PHOTO

Through Kole-Kole Pass in the Waianae Mountains flew formations of attacking Japanese planes. This view westward is toward Kepuhi Point, the site of international surfing meets.

More than 26,280 names are inscribed on the walls of the
"Courts of the Missing" at the National Memorial
Cemetery of the Pacific, on Oahu.

carrots, but couldn't export acres of rotting egg plant. It also possessed no sugar, flour or coffee. Kauai ran out of butter, rice and meat.

Hawaii and Maui were lucky in that they raised cattle and grew vegetables in great quantities. Yet these products, the mainstay of their economy, couldn't be transported to the other islands.

Inevitably, variety became a difficult problem. For example, Kauai was urged to grow potatoes to relieve a severe lack. Just as she began harvesting her crop, a huge shipment arrived from the States. Maui didn't fare too well with onions. Just as her harvest was due, three shipments, that had been ordered from the mainland for spaced delivery, arrived all at once.

Businesses also felt the impact of change. Nearly eight thousand firms or shops closed their doors in 1942. Others expanded under the specific and peculiar needs of wartime.

Kodak became a V-mail center, reducing soldiers' letters to microfilm, a process that saved transporting thousands of postal tons to the mainland. The Hawaiian Pineapple Company turned to packing assault rations. Hawaiian Gas Products began supplying chemicals for fire extinguishers, flame throwers, rubber rafts and barrage balloons.

Restauranteurs, whose trade had been wrecked by early curfews, food shortages and a lack of tourists, experienced a boom with the mass arrival of soldiers and sailors. Laundries, dry cleaners and banks were among the service businesses to inherit a bumper crop of customers, far more than they needed.

But, all firms and establishments suffered from a lack of raw material, wares and manpower—also from new government red tape and regulations.

In order to prevent vast amounts of United States currency from falling into the hands of possible invaders or being smuggled out by saboteurs, the Hawaiian government ordered a new control system. Over and above their payrolls, businesses and industries were allowed no more than $500 cash at regular intervals and private citizens, no more than $200.

A new legal tender was then designed, printed and finally issued. It was worthless anywhere else in the world, unless exchanged in Washington. And what spy wanted to do that?

The new bills somewhat resembled the old but the colors were altered and they carried the imprint "HAWAII" prominently on the face. In a way, then, the tender became authorized "counterfeits." The exchanged "old money," $200 million, was burned in the crematory of Nuuanu Cemetery.

All of the ships which had once carried luxury trade from the Pacific coast had sailed off to war in deepest gray. The largest of the area's steamship companies, the Matson Line, converted her four beautiful passenger lines into transports which brought troops and ammunition from the mainland. On the return voyages, they took dependents, the sick and the wounded. Matson freighters hauled ammunition, medical supplies, guns and other military equipment not only in the wide Pacific, but also on other seas—from Murmansk to Madagascar.

Many of the tugs, barges and interisland vessels of Hawaii were taken over by the United States Engineers and converted for sea duty. One steamship, owned by the Commercial Pacific Cable Company, became an important communications link in the Pacific for the Signal Corps. Even the tuna boats were commandeered for patrol and they were well-adapted to the rough seas that were so frequently a backdrop for their duty.

On March 3, the Japanese executed a poor encore of their December performance. Two long-range, 4-engine flying boats droned in at 15,000 feet, from Wotje, in the Marshalls, refueling from a submarine at desolate French Frigate Shoals. Bad weather, coupled with searchlights and effective antiaircraft, chased the two intruders off. The pilots dropped their bombs harmlessly in the hills of Oahu and in the sea.

The early months of 1942, however, continued overwhelmingly in favor of the enemy. The battle of the Java Sea, the greatest naval fight since Jutland in 1916, commencing February 27 and continuing for three days, had cost a combined American, British, Australian and Dutch fleet five cruisers, including President Roosevelt's favorite *Houston*, thirteen destroyers, plus the ancestral carrier *Langley*, the Navy oiler *Pecos* and two destroyers in related actions.

Not one Japanese warship had been sunk or seriously damaged.

Six weeks later, on April 18, Colonel James Doolittle led sixteen Army bombers off the decks of the carrier *Hornet* to bomb Tokyo and other targets in Japan. A token raid, it helped morale on the United States home front but proved of little military significance.

The Navy was faced thereby with an even greater lack of ships. The loss of the Philippines with the surrender of Corregidor on May 6 and of the carrier *Lexington* two days later in the battle of the Coral Sea demonstrated as well the need for carriers and transports to build up supply lines to distant outposts. Hong Kong, Singapore and the Dutch East Indies were now occupied by the Japanese. A foothold had been wrested by the enemy in the Northern Solomons and New Guinea.

Meanwhile, Navy intelligence learned of a major assault brewing within the Japanese Imperial High Command, which believed that the bombers of Doolittle's strike on Tokyo were land-based somewhere in the Pacific. The enemy, not knowing that these bombers were launched from the carrier *Hornet*, finally decided Midway, or "AF" as the Japanese called it in code, was the stronghold that now needed to be captured.

Since the Japanese naval code had been cracked, it was known that an attack was being planned. But was "AF" the code name for Midway—or Hawaii? Worried, Admiral Nimitz immediately left Hawaii and flew to Midway.

A Navy intelligence officer, Commander Joseph Rochefort, came up with an idea. He asked Midway to transmit an uncoded radio message to the effect that trouble was being experienced with water distillation. The ruse worked. Two days later, Tokyo noted that "AF" was running short of fresh water. The date was also revealed: June 3.

Nimitz returned to Hawaii where he organized two task forces. These comprised three aircraft carriers, *Enterprise*, *Hornet* and *Yorktown*, supported by eight cruisers and fifteen destroyers. The *Yorktown* was barely repaired from her damage at Coral Sea. The air power which Nimitz assembled had to come in from all directions and from the three different services, the Navy, Army and Marines. Midway itself counted 120 planes, some of which were obsolete bombers or old patrol-boats. Nevertheless, when the carrier squadrons were totalled up, the United States was able to go into battle with 415 fighters, bombers, torpedo and reconnaissance aircraft.

The Japanese fleet moving toward Midway comprised eleven battleships, nine carriers, fourteen cruisers, forty-seven destroyers, nine supply ships and twelve transports, carrying roughly three thousand troops. The main striking force was under the direction of Vice Admiral Chuichi Nagumo, who had commanded the Pearl Harbor fleet.

The battle that began on June 3 became one of the most decisive in history. Waged by carrier planes and land-based bombers, the struggle raged for three days. Admiral of the Fleet Isoroku Yamamoto, at 2:55 A.M., June 5, ordered the occupation of "AF" cancelled and the great force to retire.

Japan had lost four carriers, a heavy cruiser, 250 planes and more than two thousand men, at a cost to the United States of one carrier, the *Yorktown*, one destroyer, 150 planes and three hundred men. Midway was superficially damaged.

For once the Pacific pushed the European war news off the front page. The *Star-Bulletin* on June 5 blared in three-inch letters: JAPANESE AT MIDWAY SMASHED; and the Honolulu *Advertiser*, June 7, read: JAPANESE NAVY CUT IN HALF.

When Admiral Nimitz had wrested Midway from Tokyo's grasp, he punned: "Perhaps we will be forgiven if we claim that we are about midway to our objective."

The United States had a top secret and emergency "crash" plan to leave the vital island of Oahu "scorched." Any building or facility which could be used militarily was to be blasted into rubble to deter an invader from setting foot upon this bit of American soil. After Midway, it was apparent that the plan could be catalogued into a semiactive file.

As Ensign Toshio Hashimoto, one of Japan's horizontal bomber pilots on December 7, would observe: "We had caused America's darkest hour. But as the days grew into weeks and the weeks into months, the United States took on a new light and it blinded. . . ."

CHAPTER 11

Gradually, the heart of Polynesia evolved into a vast arsenal, hospital and rest area as well as a stage for the invasions to come. Twelve Army infantry and three Marine divisions, involving more than a million men, would ultimately train in the Islands.

Hawaii counted three divisions of its own: the 7th, 24th and 25th. One of the regiments of the 7th had been commissioned at Schofield Barracks in honor of Queen Liliuokalani in 1916, the year before her death. "The Queen's Own Regiment," along with the other divisions, was specifically charged with the defense of the Islands. It would see action along the watery road to Tokyo with the 25th at Guadalcanal, the 24th at New Guinea, the 7th in the Philippines and the 25th and 24th as well.

To Kauai, small and isolated to the west, the 27th Division was a "savior." The inhabitants actually succeeded in bringing their "adopted" division back after service in the Marshalls-Gilberts campaign, but they would lose the 27th again to the mounting conflict.

Hawaii had at least a glimpse of every type of fighting man, as well as the women to back them up: nurses, Waves, WAC's, Lady Marines, Red Cross "gals" and the legions of entertainers sponsored by the USO and other organizations.

There were "flyboys," a devil-may-care breed not unlike their daddies in the first war; the more phlegmatic submariners; ranger-type foot soldiers who took a page or two from the lore of the American Indian; the tough, sturdy tank crewmen who appeared to the Hawaiians worthy of the tradition of Kamehameha's warriors; the mathematically-inclined heavy artillery experts who believed that big blasts and enough of them were about all that was needed to win the war.

Unique among all these rapidly accumulating and diverse forces were the frogmen.

These broad-shouldered, full-chested, husky young men, who already were capturing imaginations back home, arrived on Maui from basic training at Fort Pierce, Florida, where the water temperature and surf were similar. Those who could not swim at least a mile carrying heavy equipment flunked out.

They readied for the Fifth Amphibious Force, under Admiral Turner, the same hard-bitten officer who had been Chief of War Plans. Those who blueprinted Underwater Demolition Teams had thrown away the books. Anything went.

One swimmer, rehearsing on little Kahoolawe Island, south of Maui, protested a 9 A.M. takeoff time for the real invasion: "You don't swim into somebody's beach in broad daylight, sir!"

He was rebuffed by Admiral Turner, "You do!" And that was that.

They *did* in island after island, on the long, tough sea road back to Tokyo. Losses were light in proportion to the grave risks confronting the frogmen. Skill and endurance were their armor.

Pilots and submariners were more familiar to Hawaiians than the frogmen. The former had the use of a mansion on Kalakaua Avenue, the latter the Royal Hawaiian Hotel. The Breakers, on Waikiki Beach, was leased as a rest-stop for soldier and sailor alike, while the Haleiwa Hotel gleamed under a "brassier" patronage. Doris Duke donated her mansion to staff officers.

Lodgings during leaves at all of these places were free to weary and funseeking enlisted personnel and at a nominal sum to officers. Fort de Russey, equipped with swimming pools, a ballroom, barracks and dining halls, was converted into a vast recreation complex.

A "Serviceman's Calendar" ran in the Maui *News*, calling attention to such events as: "today—Army Band Concert at Alexander House Patio, 4 to 5 P.M.; Parties: an all day party, with everything supplied for the first twenty-five servicemen to register at the Wailuku, USO Center." Fifty similar centers were established by the USO throughout the Islands.

The Army Special Services and the Navy Recreation and Morale Office sponsored their own shows, sports events, libraries, radio stations and newspapers. Stars from the athletic and entertainment world were frequent visitors.

Everything possible was done to try to encourage servicemen to stay away from the gambling places, bars and other tawdry Loreleis on Hotel Street and similar byways of the city's red light district. Vice and racketeering was at times so bad, in fact, that unscrupulous hucksters attempted to sell gold stars to mothers, hinting that their sons were dead.

One celebrity, Eleanor Roosevelt, returning from a Pacific tour in the fall of 1943, met her old friend Judith Anderson, the actress, and

Maurice Evans, who were performing in *Macbeth*.

"Some of the soldiers," Miss Anderson confided to the President's wife, "had never been to the theater before. One of them asked me, 'Who's this guy Shakespeare?' "

At the Royal Hawaiian, the First Lady carried her own tray in the cafeteria line. She did borrow a maid from Governor Ingram Stainback. While there she was asked if she thought the men in the Pacific were possibly "pampered" or, on the other extreme, afforded insufficient comfort. Mrs. Roosevelt thought, then wryly replied, "Neither." And that enigmatic answer concluded the conversation.

Of all the comings and goings during the war, those of the submarine service were surely among the most dramatic, if unheralded.

"We could see them slide into the harbor occasionally," wrote Robert Casey, a correspondent, "salt-caked, battered and ugly-looking, long black sewer pipes covered with patches of white. We were struck by the pomp and circumstance of their arrival, with a busy-looking fourpiper [a World War I vintage destroyer] ahead and sometimes another behind them."

The men were just as grimy as their submarines. They looked at land, at food and at women as though seeing them all for the first time. A group who called themselves the Waikiki Hostesses hauled the underseas crews through a whirl of dances, dinners and all sorts of parties. Before the boats slipped out of Pearl Harbor, the men were given sweaters and warm socks, knitted by the Red Cross.

By the end of 1943, five new submarines a month, with mother ship tenders, were passing through Hawaii for final training before having "a go" at the enemy.

The waters offshore were not themselves wholly free of Japanese submarines, although they were never present in numbers. They maintained reconnaissance, observing fleet target practice and noting convoys and task forces. Suspected silhouettes or underwater echoes were the targets of frequent depth chargings and aerial bombardment.

As a Navy pilot observed, "Them's were bad times for whales."

Late in October, 1943, a submarine-launched enemy plane flew over Oahu. Undetected until captured records would reveal its presence, the pilot returned to report "the major part" of the fleet was absent from Pearl Harbor. This was true enough. The Navy was busy much closer to the flier's home islands.

This same fall, Hawaiians of Japanese ancestry who had been in the Engineers were formed into the 100th Infantry Battalion and sent into their first major action in Europe at Salerno. They were attached to the 34th "Red Bull" Infantry Division, which was generally made up of tall soldiers of Scandinavian ancestry from Minnesota, Iowa and North and South Dakota.

Retired Infantry Colonel Robert V. Shinn, then a battalion executive officer in the 34th, remembers the little Hawaiians on whom "the long, full infantry combat pack almost touched the ground."

"There was a lot of good-natured kidding between these two groups, the Swedes suggesting to the Hawaiians that they needed roller skates to carry their packs. But we found them fearless fighters, as proven by their casualty record. Among their deeds of valor, I remember best that they used to swarm over the dreaded German 'Tiger' tanks, pry open their hatches and hurl hand grenades in them."

The shortage of manpower in the Islands grew more acute. Every able-bodied citizen, male and female, was urged to work. Newspapers criticized anyone who didn't do so as a "loafer." The pressure was so great in fact that many who logged full-time employment sought also part-time. Even the soldiers and sailors were latching onto extra jobs. Some were waiting on tables, driving trucks, even teaching school.

All women over sixteen had been required early in the war to register. Soon, half of the female population of Hawaii was employed, the remainder being disabled, or engaged in the care of small children or invalids. Ultimately, the labor force throughout the Islands expanded to 1 ¼ million.

"So great has been the influx of people that our streets are teeming with milling throngs of war workers and service personnel of both sexes," wrote Sister Adele Marie, of the Order of St. Joseph of Carondelet, a teacher. "The problems arising from housing conditions have become acute. On every available site a mushroom growth of buildings has sprung up—buildings for the use of the armed forces or for the newly-arrived citizens. Island terrain is thickly dotted with countless town-sized encampments of Quonset huts, army tents, wooden shacks or rambling barracks.

"I almost dislike going to town these days. Honolulu, with its boomtown aspect, is battening in a sea of feverish activity. The easy-going tenor of bygone days is no more. Prosperity is leaving a spirit of sophisticated modernity in its wake."

The trade in souvenirs alone grew into a $5 million a year business.

"Prior to the war," according to Sister Adele, "we had about ninety-five stores in Honolulu which specialized in Hawaiian curios; now we have nearly three hundred. The amusing side of it all is that over 80 per cent of our 'Hawaiian curios' are manufactured in the States. . . ."

The number of help-wanted ads in the Hawaiian newspapers soared. It was not unusual to see the same ones repeated week after week. The Hawaiian Tuna Packers, Ltd., long since converted to making components for Navy combat planes, was typical in not including the word "skilled" in ads, knowing there would be few if any applicants if they did so.

The newspapers had long since returned to running the funny papers and cartoons, but the humor was vastly different. A typical cartoon showed one guest at a wedding saying to another: "They met on the assembly line . . . it was love at first bomb sight."

As the "Rock," as the GIs called Oahu, mushroomed in importance, the Hawaiian Department was designated in August, 1943, "Headquarters, United States Army Forces, Central Pacific Area."

In late 1943, a huge amphibious force, which had trained for many months in Hawaii, sailed for the major battle of Tarawa. Two of the three battleships lending cover to the troops on the morning of November 19 were of special interest. If ships can have memories, two had long ones, the *Maryland* and the *Tennessee*.

From December, 1943, to December, 1944, American and Australian troops advanced westward from New Guinea. Steadily, the Allies battled their way, island by island, from Hawaii toward Japan.

Then, one midafternoon, May 21, 1944, residents for many miles around the naval base had reason to believe that Oahu had once again been attacked. Explosions rattled doors and windows as columns of flame and smoke towered skyward from Pearl Harbor.

A landing ship tank (LST) unloading 4.2-caliber mortar shells had caught fire and blown up. The conflagration quickly spread to other vessels in the West Loch anchorage. According to John T. Sawyer, coxswain on the LST 480: "I was standing midship on the starboard side. It knocked me on the deck and about the time I got up, pieces were burning all over the main deck of the ship. I went over to the port side and turned the fire hose on and was spraying water all over the main deck . . . then the next ship blew up and I went back aft and was helping get the lines off aft. When we got them off, the 480 was burning forward and then there was a big explosion. It knocked me over the side and when I reached the beach, I looked back and I could see the rest of the crew jumping over the side."

Troops on many of the ships leaped overboard, onto piers, waiting boats and into the Loch itself. A large ammunition depot on shore was threatened, but the main damage consisted of broken windows.

A Liberty ship, carrying three thousand tons of ammunition, caught fire, but by fast work her crew brought the flames under control. Most of the LSTs were too badly damaged to permit fireline pressure. Captain Francis S. Craven, captain of the Pearl Harbor Navy Yard, ordered two carriers, anchored nearby, to sea.

Performing a daring job, yard tugs towed two lighters, loaded with nearly one thousand tons of powder, to a far anchorage. One large tug hauled a smaller one, wedged between two burning LSTs, to safety.

When the fire finally burned out the next morning, the total damage could be assessed. Four officers and 123 enlisted had been killed; nearly four hundred were injured. Six LSTs were destroyed and three LCTs (Landing craft, tank), which had been aboard the large landing craft, along with them. Six yard tugs were damaged. Sabotage was hinted, but never proven. The Court of Inquiry, which fixed no guilt, suggested that gasoline vapors may have become ignited, in turn firing the mortar shells.

In July, 1944, Pearl Harbor became the site of one of President Roosevelt's several fateful meetings. He conferred with Nimitz and General MacArthur aboard the cruiser *Birmingham*, on final Pacific strategy. Possible invasions of China and Formosa figured prominently in the discussions, but General MacArthur strongly objected. He favored a thrust toward the Philippines.

After the meeting with President Roosevelt, MacArthur, driving through Oahu's "multitude of camps," was shocked to observe that his Commander in Chief was "just a shell of a man I had known. It was clearly evident that his days were numbered." Shortly after Roosevelt's return to Washington, the potential China offensive was cancelled and the troops from Hawaii headed for Iwo Jima and, eventually, Okinawa.

By the end of 1944, the Allies had pushed the Japanese out of most of the island barriers east and south of Japan. New Guinea, the Admiralties, Solomons, the Marianas, most of the Marshalls, the Carolines and much of the Philippines were once more in friendly hands.

During the invasion at Leyte in the Philippines the destroyer *Ward* was hit by a Kamikaze on her port side and sunk. Captain Wallace S. Wharton noted: "It was an odd turn of fate that arranged that this should occur on December 7, 1944, the very anniversary of her having fired the first shot from a U.S. Naval vessel in the war against Japan, at Pearl Harbor, December 7, 1941."

Using Saipan in the Marianas as a base, the Air Force now began to "soften up" Japan with massive bombing raids. At first the Americans bombed by day, but in January, 1945, they changed tactics and bombed by night with fire bombs. The 7th Air Force, which had so long operated out of Hawaii, moved to Saipan, and then on to Okinawa.

Attacking forces set out in early January, 1945, for Iwo Jima and at the same time, Admiral Nimitz transferred his headquarters westward from Hawaii to Guam to be near the theater of operation.

In January, 1945, Sister Adele Marie wrote: "Perhaps the saddest spots on our horizons are those numerous and hivelike hospitals into which pour a constant stream of war casualties. Honolulu has seen the real heroes of Tarawa, Kwajalein, Saipan, Tinian and Iwo Jima; the men whose mangled bodies have been reduced to human torsoes and who are known in hospital parlance as 'basket cases'. . . ."

On May 8, 1945, VE Day was proclaimed in Europe, to be followed by a swift chain of events. On June 21, the Battle of Okinawa ended in decisive victory. On July 4, General MacArthur announced the liberation of the Philippines, in toto.

Japan had yet to be crushed once and for all within her home islands. On August 6, the United States dropped an atomic bomb on Hiroshima; three days later, another on Nagasaki. These two terrible missiles forced Japan into unconditional surrender and ushered in a new and fearful age of man.

Formal surrender terms were signed upon the battleship *Missouri* in Tokyo Bay on September 2. Alongside was the *West Virginia*, risen from the humiliation and wreckage of Pearl Harbor.

Other ships had returned from December 7 to give good accounting of themselves; the *Nevada* was present at the invasion of Normandy; the *California* took part in seven Pacific battles. Among the large war vessel casualties of Pearl Harbor, only the *Arizona*, *Oklahoma* and *Utah* would never raise anchor again.

CHAPTER 12

The Monday after the surrender, which happened to be Labor Day, Honolulu turned out for a victory parade. Tens of thousands of its citizens rode flower-decorated floats; others marched or applauded from the sidewalks. Airplanes formed an honor guard in the skies.

"At long last," wrote Sister Adele, "VJ Day has come. It is the eve of Mary's feast and the heart of a war-torn world sings with the Queen of Heaven.

"Yet despite the cessation of hostilities there is a feeling of apprehension in the air. In its wake the war has left ghastly scars and a foul leaven whose taint obscures the rays of peace."

Peace returned to the Pacific and to a Hawaii which would never be the same. On the priority list was demobilization. Men in uniform were satisfied with transportation home aboard anything which floated, even sampans if such should be specified on their travel orders. Some offered a whole year's pay for a seat on an airplane or an upper bunk on a transport, but there was none for sale at any price.

The *Saratoga*, which had missed most of the fighting, steamed east bearing four thousand servicemen to "processing" centers which in a few minutes could transform them into civilians again.

In October, the 4th Marines, bedecked with leis, listened to their last alohas as they left Maui. Tent cities, Quonset huts and other temporary structures which had caught MacArthur's notice began to melt, leaving grass and fields, empty concrete, asphalt plazas and byroads.

There was some trouble as more impatient soldiers, sailors or airmen wondered why their turn at repatriation had not come. England, France and Germany had much the same problem.

By the spring of 1946, however, almost all of the war "crew" had quit the Pacific. Fresh occupation units now unrolled their bedding on the newly-won islands and in Japan. They joined some five thousand Americans from the mainland who remained as civilians to take jobs or open businesses. Not a few found the Hawaiian girls irresistible and married them.

Reconversion of war plants commenced, although some former peacetime premises had been so worn or damaged as to be useless. Indemnities had to be arranged. Disposal of war surplus was a lingering concern. Warehouses from Honolulu to Tokyo bulged with military supplies earmarked for a war that was over.

Over a three-year period a giant grab-bag assortment of used military "hardware," from jeeps and airplanes to tooth brushes and complete field kitchens, was sold to the citizenry of the Islands and to wholesalers who had come from other places. The United Nations bought a considerable tonnage of construction equipment for China.

Some was salvaged—burned, buried or floated out to sea on barges and dumped overboard. On the less populous Pacific islands, this "junk" was abandoned to rust and weather and supply a perch for plumed native birds.

After the Pearl Harbor attack, Hawaii's destiny was woven even more tightly with that of the United States proper. People in the Islands had died, bled and sacrificed in countless ways. Full statehood did not seem too much to ask at all.

Joseph R. Farrington, Hawaii's delegate to the Congress of the United States, found that opposition centered around two principal fears or perhaps hallucinations of the lawmakers: one, the legislators did not want a state in the Union which was "dominated by Japs"; two, the labor unions were controlled by communists, who would assume too strong a role in state government.

Statehood bills passed the House of Representatives in 1947 and again in 1950. They went no further but they were a start.

In the late spring of 1950, a Constitutional Convention and an investigation of suspected subversive activities took front place among all Hawaiian thoughts and activities. The convention was formed for drawing up the entire modus operandi of statehood, looking toward Hawaii's admission to the Union. Delegates met and deliberated earnestly week after week.

Then, on June 24, 1950, word came that North Korea had invaded the Republic of Korea, which had been established but two years previously under United Nations supervision. President Harry Truman hurried military aid to the defenders even before the ponderous wheels of the UN could start to turn. On July 5 the Constitutional Convention, labor unions and other organizations, both business and professional in the Islands, endorsed the Chief

Executive's speedy response.

Hawaii, back at war again, "shook itself and tabulated once more its defenses," as the *Star-Bulletin* phrased it. The air raid warning system was hooked up, the sirens themselves dusted off and repainted. Visiting was suspended at the Naval Base and security generally tightened.

Government bond drives were reinstituted. The Hawaiian National Guard "froze" all discharges. Thirty-five mothballed ships were recommissioned at the Navy Yard, demanding, among other physical and economic considerations, 130,000 manhours in overtime pay.

The Military Air Transport Service, which had distinguished itself in the Berlin Airlift, would acknowledge more curtain calls. Soon, one of its big freighter-transports of the sky was leaving Hickam every seventy-five minutes. Within the first three months of hostilities, MATS moved eight thousand tons of rockets, 30-caliber shells, blood plasma, machine gun mounts and related materiel together with 34,000 troops into the war zone. Wounded and dependents were flown back to or through Hawaii.

Wheeler Air Force Base, partially closed in 1949, was cranked up again, to accommodate the growing MATS traffic. Among the first to land there, in July, was the *Good Hope*, chartered from Pan American Airways, carrying thirty-nine children, twenty-seven women and four servicemen. One of the women quietly identified herself as a war widow.

Red Cross Gray Ladies, whose work had never really ceased—VJ-Day was relatively recent history—simply increased their numbers to serve at the Tripler Army General Hospital and at military clinics. As in two World Wars, these volunteers shouldered much of the load of registered nurses, all the way from supervising occupational therapy classes to writing letters for the badly wounded or very ill.

Among the more tireless of the Red Cross auxiliary women were those of Korean ancestry who were particularly adept at rolling surgical bandages. The Junior Red Cross ran errands, baked cookies by the tens of thousands, crocheted slippers, carved ashtrays from coconut shells and performed countless little tasks all aimed at boosting the morale of the fighting men.

Most of those who remained any length of time in Tripler's wards were Hawaiian residents. The 5th Regimental Combat Team, for example, about four thousand officers and men, was 40 per cent Hawaiian. It had, in fact, been in Korea earlier on occupation duty. The familiar 24th Division sailed back to war in early July. It would defend the perimeter of the strategic port of Pusan, needed for future troop debarkations and cargo.

Again, the Islands experienced a shortage of skilled labor. Nearly five thousand Hawaiians who would otherwise have been qualified were on such other important advance Pacific bases as Okinawa and Guam.

Civilian defense units were reorganized along the same lines as before, involved with protection of utilities, communications and dwelling areas. There was a new ingredient added this time—What to do in case of atomic attack?—although nuclear weapons were still the exclusive property of the United States.

Prices were higher than in 1941; so were taxes. But there were no scarcities or rationings as in the early World War II years.

Hawaii now had help as a Pacific base of operations, especially from the American camps, airfields and ports in occupied Japan. The permanent population itself remained on the increase, as did the flow of industrial and professional capital from the mainland.

And, as one sociologist put it, this returned war period saw the "emergence of vocal leadership, financial, political and professional among the citizens of Asian ancestry." In other words, the conflict in Korea notwithstanding, the 1950's were a vigorous growth time.

It was quite true that native-born soldiers suffered a much higher casualty rate than in the 1941-45 span. The daily press attested to this.

". . . 80 of us went and 30 of us came back," Private First Class Harold Hunter, of Honolulu, wrote home of an assault upon a hill.

The Teiki Miyashiro family on Kauai lost two of three sons, all in Korea. The Mokiaos, of Molokai, existed in an atmosphere of alternate hope and despair for three months as contradictory reports came back to them. Finally, there was incontestable proof: their son Corporal Raymond Mokiao was dead.

But the grief of families such as the Arakawas and Kumagals turned to rejoicing with the capture of Pyongyang, the capital of North Korea, and the discovery that their sons, listed as "missing," were alive. They had been held prisoner and were liberated by advancing UN forces.

While the fighting slackened in mid-1952 as truce talks commenced, the armistice was not signed at Panmunjom until July 27, 1953. The war, an especially horrible and dirty one, had lasted three years, one month and two days. The United Nations forces counted 74,000 dead, 250,000 wounded and 83,000 missing or captured. The American toll represented nearly one-half the overall figures.

Civilians continued the inhuman twentieth century tradition of being the hardest hit: 400,000 dead, by estimates.

"We have won an armistice on a single battle front, not peace in the world," asserted war-wise President Eisenhower. "We may not relax our guard nor cease our quest."

And again the quest for statehood became the foremost concern. In March, 1959, both the House and Senate passed an enabling act by a 4-1 majority. A plebiscite in the Islands ratified the measure on June 28. On August 21, Eisenhower proclaimed Hawaii the fiftieth state in the Union.

CHAPTER 13

For more than a half century the Hawaiian Islands had proven an increasingly important segment of the United States. Already a helpmate through six wars or "actions," they were, as well, important to the national economy.

Full statehood for such a small parcel of land, especially one separated by more than two thousand miles of water, is unique. But these islands constitute an exceptional state, populated by exceptional people. They more than earned the privilege of statehood.

Today, nearly 850,000 persons call Hawaii home. This represents an increase of more than 200,000 in a decade. All but approximately 135,000 reside in Oahu. Truly an integrated culture, the population is 38 per cent Caucasian, 29 per cent Japanese and the remainder of other Oriental origins.

In testament to youth, the median age is just slightly over twenty-four, approximately five years younger than the national average. At twenty, a resident can vote in the local elections, that is, for the governor or lieutenant governor as well as for the twenty-five members of the state Senate or fifty-one members of the House of Representatives.

The robust growth of Oahu is immediately apparent to anyone landing at Honolulu International Airport, which handles more than four million passengers annually and nearly forty-one million pounds of cargo, plus twelve million pounds of mail.

The bright-colored, sprawling city of Honolulu, which accounts for nearly half of the entire population of the Islands, would scarcely be recognizable to a Japanese pilot of December 7, except for such principal landmarks as Diamond Head, the Aloha Tower or, at a lower altitude, the Iolani Palace.

Gone are the trolley cars, the old two- and three-story hotels and most of the shabby store fronts associated with the early 1940's. A construction boom to the total tab of nearly a half billion dollars has sent modern glass and stainless steel or aluminum office buildings and high-rise apartments skyward.

Slender cranes swing and turn astride fresh foundations seemingly on every other city block of Honolulu. Suburbia keeps stretching out over the ridges toward all of Oahu's four coasts, just as in the environs of "mainland" America. The contrast lies in airy construction, lack of basements and, often, dining room or living room windows.

There is also a vast difference in price. For a house in the posh purlieus of Kaneohe Bay or along the spectacular Nuuanu Pali—any figure up to $100,000. A comparable home on the mainland, even with heating, storm windows and perhaps a basement, might be one-third or even one-half less than in Hawaii.

Hawaii, by any yardstick, is an expensive place to live. It is exceeded only by Juneau, Alaska, and ranks with Washington, D.C., where only the most frugal can boast they are ahead after the last nickel is taken out of the monthly pay check.

Inflation, of course, is among the reasons. Builders blame soaring costs on the necessity of freighting virtually every pound of materials from the west coast. Food is proportionately dear. Poi is scarce at 42¢ a pound. Aku, Hawaiian bonito, is $1.19 a pound, if obtainable. The cost of dinner at an average restaurant for which one might pay $4.00 or $5.00 in Chicago would be $8.00 or more in Waikiki or elsewhere.

Automobiles rank with family jewels. They can be traded and resold until they just about fall apart. More than 300,000 are registered in Hawaii; new or used, they command prices sometimes nearly double what they are worth on the mainland.

The inhabitants, offered scanty public transport, need their own conveyances. Oahu has approximately twelve thousand miles of paved roads, including the dual-lane superhighways, Kamehameha—"Kam" —Moanalua, Lunalilo, Likelike and Pali. The old chieftains would not believe their eyes could they return and look at the traffic.

Hawaii, the "big island," has about two hundred miles more of roads than Oahu, but since Hawaii also records a circumference approximately three times that of Oahu, this fact is not surprising.

On the bottom of the scale is little Lanai, west of Oahu and wholly owned by the Dole Pineapple Company, with fifty miles of surfaced roads and 773 registered vehicles. No automobiles were registered on Lanai before 1958.

Driving in Hawaii, in spite of an evident constabulary, can be compared to France, Germany and Italy, where it is a case of everyone for himself. As the military bases open up their many gates around 3:30 P.M., "Kam" highway is bumper to bumper. Fender bending is much more the rule than the exception.

On Sundays, the same highways become speedways as the citizens swarm toward the west coast for surfboarding or to the even greater profusion of beaches on the windier eastern shores. The northern perimeter, around Kahuku Point, offers narrow, winding access. One hesitant lady or one truck can and regularly does cause traffic jams of monumental significance.

Obviously, to sustain an increasingly comfortable if not quite champagne standard of living, money flourishes in these islands. Total personal income is in the neighborhood of $2.5 billion, with its rate of increase and per capita somewhat above the national averages. Unemployment has dropped to about 3.5 per cent of the normal labor market, about half that on the mainland.

Defense expenditures continue as Hawaii's greatest source of revenue. This has been $600 million annually, although cutbacks on a broad scale are rapidly reducing this particular cornucopia.

Tourism ranks next, with approximately $400 million being pumped into the state's economy each year. Sugar and pineapple production combined account for about one-third of a billion dollars.

"Heavy" and even "light" industry is not associated with Hawaii. Nonetheless, both categories of nonagricultural manufacture exist, with a combined value of more than $200 million. A petroleum refinery, two cement plants, a rolling mill, concrete plant, flour mill and plastics factory have recently opened.

Ninety garment manufacturers, several textile and conventional printing plants, plastic processors and furniture makers are among the "light" category.

Education, on an upsurge ever since the days of the missionaries, still flourishes. There are 207 public and 98 private educational institutions in Hawaii, with a total enrollment of 202,839. The University of Hawaii, state-controlled, has its main campus in Honolulu, with a branch in Hilo—for a total student body of nearly twenty thousand. Bachelor degrees are offered in sixty-five fields, masters in sixty-seven and doctorates in twenty-seven.

This beautiful place of higher learning is located on the northeast side of Honolulu at the foot of the Waahila Ridge. One of Oahu's showplaces, its broad lawns, tropical trees and bright flowers make it distinctive among American colleges and universities.

Its East-West Center was launched in 1960 with a $10 million appropriation from Congress, wholly international in purpose and scope, attracting students from Asia, Southeast Asia and the rest of the world.

The university also sponsors a Theater Group, which makes a

notable contribution to the artistic community. Other cultural activities include an eighty-five-piece symphony, a community theater, Magic Ring Theater, the Windward Theater Guild and numerous art groups.

The John F. Kennedy Theater is surpassed in size only by Honolulu's new International Center, with a two-thousand-seat theater and concert hall plus an eight-thousand-seat arena.

Four smaller private colleges, one private junior college and five public two-year community colleges together with several business and technical schools complete Hawaii's broad and diverse offerings in the world of education.

The Bishop Museum is well known for its extensive collection of European, Oriental and Hawaiian art and its sponsoring of courses. Other museums are located on Kauai, Maui and at Hilo, Hawaii.

The most spectacular attraction of all, the Volcanoes National Park, is on the "Big Island." Mauna Loa is the world's most active volcano. Nearby Mauna Kea at 13,796 feet is the highest peak in the Pacific.

The smaller Kilauea volcano erupted with sufficient power in 1790 to wipe out part of the army of a local king, Keoua. What are supposed to be the footprints of these hapless soldiers are timelessly preserved in the long-hardened lava flow.

For those who make the approximately two-hundred-mile journey from Honolulu to the "Big Island," the volcanoes are an outstanding attraction. These craters are also "safe," since they do not spew forth the more common and often fatal clouds of ash. Also, moving lava streams cool rather quickly.

Hawaii, with a few exceptions, is considered an exceptionally healthy place to live. The Islands are among the very few areas on earth free of rabies, malaria, dengue fever, yellow fever, filariasis (elephantiasis) and cholera. No case of smallpox has been reported since 1913.

The one exception is leprosy, now known as Hansen's Disease, named after the Norwegian, Henrik Hansen, who isolated the bacillus involved one hundred years ago. However, the infection today can be arrested through the use of sulphur drugs, combined with surgery as necessary. There is still a "settlement" hospital on Molokai and another in Honolulu, with a combined capacity of three hundred beds.

The State Health Department, the oldest in the United States, was founded in 1850 by King Kamehameha III. More than half of the thirty-nine hospitals on the Islands are accredited by the American Hospital Association. They feature the principal specializations, from obstetrics to mental health.

Vietnam necessarily commands the major focus of the United States Pacific Command's ("PACOM's") planning, coordination and logistics at the present time. Communications, for example, is a booming "industry" in Hawaii, especially on the island of Oahu, which bristles with many types of antennae. Wheeler and Bellows Air Force Bases have virtually been turned into vast transmitting and relay centers.

The Army privates on Opana Point who watched in disbelief as the shower of "blips" heralded the approach of the Japanese attackers in 1941 would not recognize the massive saucer-type receivers on the same location. They are just part of the awesome gadgetry of Communications Satellite Corporation.

"Stratcompac" is but one of the numerous tags for the several armed services' communications systems represented in Hawaii. This one happens to be an Army nerve network originating in Fort Huachuca, Arizona.

By the same token, electronics is a top-ranking skill here. The Signal Corps of the Army and sister branches of the Navy and Air Force are well represented in the Islands.

As well as the "nonoperational" mission of the armed forces in Hawaii, the physical aspects, too, have changed since World War II. However, the church-tower-like water tank at Hickam, the spacious parade ground at Shafter flanking senior officers' "country" and the barracks quadrangle at Schofield seem slated to remain.

At the Naval Base, battleship row still rings Ford Island. The barnacled, square mooring jetties dot the island's shore like derelict signposts. No battleship has tied up there since December 7, 1941.

Wreckage strews the muddy bottom, with the half-sunken, rusted *Utah* resting grotesquely on the far side of the island. Her abandonment still vexes those who once served upon her and think that she deserves a memorial similar to the glistening white marble atop the *Arizona*.

More than one-quarter million people annually visit the shrine to the ship which suffered so disproportionately. "Out of a complement of 1550 men only 289 survived," they are reminded. Rusted gun tubs remain sentry-like partly above water, with the entire silhouette, from stem to stern, visible just under the surface, to which bunker oil still bubbles up year after year.

On a broad Italian marble wall at the far end of the mausoleum-like memorial are the names of the dead and "missing." This most solemn of American shrines several times inspired the bitter retort from former President Harry Truman when the nation was condemned for dropping the atomic bomb: "But how about all those boys *down* on the *Arizona*?"

Ford Island itself is alone with its memories, a golf course, living quarters and the anti-submarine warfare headquarters. The old hangars remain, but are abandoned. Their loose sidings creak and rattle with the wind in a kind of muted dirge to so many who died in their shadows. The airstrip has become a favorite launching site for model airplanes.

Aside from an infrequent supply ship, a ferry boat to the base proper is about the only vessel which ever ties up to Ford Island, with all of its latent menace to navigation and tragic memories of yesterday.

Important as it was to Japanese gunners on December 7, this island, the old Luke Field, plays a very minor role in any of the fifty Navy commands in Hawaii—which, as a matter of fact, encompass some 33,000 officers and men and 12,000 civilians.

Across the channel, the dry dock in which the *Pennsylvania* was damaged and the *Cassin* and *Downes* ruined remains much in service, although extensively refurbished. As an old boatswain remarked, "How 'n hell can you sink a dry dock?" Of course, the enemy could and did if the dock happened to be of the floating variety.

The famous "1010" dock (1010 feet long) also resisted the on-slaught and still ties up three or four destroyers at a time, if need be, or two cruisers. The function of the Naval Base is much the same as it was on December 7, except that its transient ships are far different in character.

There are no battleships to be refueled, rearmed, and reprovisioned, and fewer cruisers and carriers than before. The destroyers, bristling with missile launchers and radar, not only bear little resemblance to their ancestors but are as large as yesterday's cruisers.

Submarines, both nuclear and nonnuclear, the pampered darlings of the fleet, are perhaps the most numerous visitors today. These underwater monsters, thirty of which are home-ported at Pearl, no longer arrive with brooms lashed to their conning towers to signify a clean sweep of the enemy. In fact, there probably wouldn't be any attachment place on the sleek conning towers with their whale fins.

Crews, however, continue to have the best of lodgings, food and recreation, including two private swimming pools. Attendants jump when the "sub boys" come ashore.

The vast Pearl Harbor complex, which is at least as important as Norfolk or San Diego, is the only military area on the island where security is still a byword: no cameras, no obvious drawing pads, visitors' permits for automobiles. The Navy obviously has not forgotten Yoshikawa and spies like him.

However, visitors can get out of their automobiles on the "Kam" Highway at Aiea or Pearl City Heights and, with the aid of even a cheap telescopic lens, take pictures of the base in the most intimate and compromising detail.

Important as Pearl Harbor is today to the Navy it may soon play a leading role in the Pacific if the Yokosuka installation in Japan is abandoned, bowing to pressure by that government.

The Navy's neighbor, Hickam Air Force Base, is equally on center stage so far as the nation's defense scheme in this part of the world is concerned. "Crossroads of the world-wide missions of the Air Force," and the second largest command in the United States' formal air arm, Hickam is headquarters of the Pacific Air Forces. The latter is composed of more than 190,000 military and civilian personnel serving in tactical, strike, support and air defense squadrons operating out of thirty-one air bases in the Pacific and Asia.

Hickam is the busy home of nearly one hundred tenant organizations, including units of the Airlift Command, Air Rescue Center and all-weather interceptor units of the Hawaii Air National Guard. The Guard is charged with the full responsibility for primary interception in the air defense of Hawaii, the only state in the Union with this arrangement. It flies Convair F-102 Delta Dagger jet interceptors.

The 61st Military Airlift Support Wing is among the busiest members of the Air Force "family" in the Islands. The freight terminal alone handles sixty thousand tons of cargo annually. The passenger terminal processes an average in excess of a half million troops and passengers each year through Hickam and adjacent Honolulu International Airport, with interlinking runways. The state, for example, owns half of the 2½-mile-long main runway.

The Pacific Military Airlift Command—"MAC"—route spans a superhighway in the skies connecting California bases through Honolulu to much of the East and Far East.

Wounded servicemen from southeast Asia are "air-evac'd" through here approximately twice a week. The patients usually continue on to the mainland, since the Army's Tripler is used for Hawaiian area needs and the Navy's "Hospital Point," off which the *Nevada* paused in her heroic dash for the open ocean, no longer lists a hospital.

There's also a "good samaritan" squadron—air rescue and recovery —working out of Hickam. The pilots' mission is to shepherd ships and aircraft in distress, military or civilian, of any nation.

The field is a "good samaritan" in other ways—reception center for the "R and R," rest and recuperation flights, which have been winging in twice a day from Vietnam to give men on the front line a brief glimpse of the good life before their tours are over. More than one-quarter million officers and men have taken advantage of these oasis trips in two years.

The facilities of Fort de Russey, in Waikiki, still are used extensively by servicemen on this type of leave. But they spell good news, too, to all of Hawaii, since the average transient spends about $800 in five days.

Hickam continues in military importance. Wheeler and Bellows are largely "bedding" areas, with much of their airstrips crisscrossed by a forest of communication towers and wires.

Were Mrs. Frank Ostenberg to revisit Wheeler she would find the then-young monkey pod trees dominating the living quarters like monster umbrellas. The click and tumble from the bowling alley and the shouts from an adjoining gymnasium, the most popular combined building at Wheeler, fill the sound void left by airplane propellers.

A riding academy is another attraction at this base once so badly handled by the Japanese. Perhaps the strongest reminder of their unwelcome visit is the exhibit of an airplane that wasn't there at all in 1941! It's a P-40 pursuit mockup used in shooting a motion picture of the Pearl Harbor attack.

Next door, Schofield Barracks remains a large garrison post with drill and firing ranges still extending to the north and east coasts. Stretching out to the west shore of Oahu, on the other side of the spectacular Waianae Ridge, is a vast ammunition dump, rumored to aggregate some millions of tons.

Schofield, headquarters for the United States Army in Hawaii, hosts presently only one combat outfit, the 4th Brigade of the 25th Division. It can shelter and feed regiments passing through Hawaii, although if a full division suddenly pops in—a tent city will have to quarter the overflow.

Burt Lancaster, on location shortly after World War II for "From Here to Eternity," would probably conclude that the post-Spanish-American War flavor of Schofield is untainted by progress in armament or evolution in architecture. The long barracks in which Frank Sinatra, also in the cast, was bedevilled to the breaking point, are familiar in color, noise and aroma.

The two eighteen-hole golf courses which the script writers portrayed as a principal raison d'être of the Army post are busier and more fastidiously manicured than ever. Clubs thrive for officers, warrants and enlisted men, but whether Lancaster's modern counterparts still prey on the lonely wives of senior commanders remains only conjecture.

On the east coast, Bellows is today but a minor part of the Waimanalo Military Reservation, with only some fifty assigned to the old flying field. What's left of the closed runways is cracked with grass and dotted with communications antennae. Occasionally a "chopper" comes over on an exercise from nearby Kaneohe Marine Corps Air Station.

Just offshore on a line with the principal strip is the skeleton of a

B-17, testament to an unsuccessful wartime takeoff. Skin divers can easily study what's left of the old Flying Fortress.

The fields, posts and bases, however, do not reflect all the transformation to military reminders of December 7. At that time, the Punchbowl Crater, overlooking Honolulu, was a beautiful parkland and promontory. From its highest point, ships far out to sea can be seen hauling in to port. To the east, Diamond Head seems less remote.

Today, Punchbowl is the site of the National Memorial Cemetery of the Pacific. It was dedicated on September 2, 1949, the fourth anniversary of VJ-Day.

Spread across 112 acres, it is the first National Cemetery to be established in the Pacific and the largest in area of three outside of the continental United States which are supervised by the Army. Containing the remains of 19,500 dead, 13,000 from World War II, Punchbowl presently is designed for 26,800 graves.

On a series of marble memorial walls are inscribed the names of 18,093 missing in World War II, plus 8,187 from the Korean conflict. Punchbowl's Hawaiian name is "Puowaina," meaning "reverence to the highest degree to hallow," long venerated by Polynesians as a resting place for the weary. Those of Japanese descent are especially attentive, keeping graves of their own meticulously tended, trimmed and bright with constantly fresh flowers.

In many ways "Puowaina" symbolizes Hawaii, the sacrifices of its people and their long-standing bond with the Americans.

POSTSCRIPT

BY THE HONORABLE HIRAM L. FONG

SENIOR SENATOR FROM HAWAII

August 21, 1959, the day President Dwight D. Eisenhower formally proclaimed Hawaii the fiftieth state, was the day our Islands were set on an equal footing with the mainland states.

More than this, however, statehood increased Hawaii's role as a vibrant, political, economic, social and cultural crossroads of the Pacific and helped our Islands serve more effectively as a bridge of understanding between East and West.

In a world struggling with racial, religious and other deep schisms, the fiftieth state demonstrates a unique model of peace, harmony and amity among her cosmopolitan population.

This is Hawaii's role as the newest state of the Union, and a role we will jealously guard. As President Eisenhower noted, "Hawaii is a successful laboratory in human brotherhood."

In bridging the gap between the United States and the Asian people who make up half the world's population, Hawaii's East-West Center at the University of Hawaii performs a vital role.

The East-West Center is a unique institution for cultural and technical interchange between the peoples of the Occident and the Orient. In addition, Hawaii provides excellent training for Peace Corps volunteers and AID personnel bound for Asian assignments.

In the transportation field, Hawaii's strategic location has been underscored by the awarding of numerous air routes to the fiftieth state and beyond, opening up further trade, commerce, tourism and business opportunities in this largest of all oceans.

International and regional meetings for the economic development of the Pacific Basin countries are being held with increasing frequency in Hawaii. And Hawaii continues to send skilled manpower to aid developing areas like the Trust Territory of the Pacific.

The fiftieth state is forging ahead also as a Pacific science center. In the Apollo 13 moon mission and space flights before it, Hawaii contributed to the epic dramas of interplanetary travel.

In the field of marine science and technology, government, industry and the academic community are joined in expanding the oceanographic front.

Hawaii has experienced an unprecedented boom in its economy since it took its place among the forty-nine other states of the Union. Its visitor industry and tourist-related employment have flourished; personal incomes have risen more than 20 per cent; the population has grown from 640,000 to more than 800,000; substantial investments have poured in from business firms on the mainland.

While these changes have been accompanied by some problems of adjustment, Hawaii today has reached higher peaks in political and economic growth than ever before.

I believe Hawaii will play an increasingly larger role in building a thriving, peaceful Pacific community. Building such a community, wherein each man retains his identity, maintains his dignity, nurtures hope for a better life and helps bring it about is a high adventure, an adventure in which we in Hawaii are pleased to share.

Our Nation's goals in Asia are our goals worldwide—self-determination and territorial integrity for nations large and small; opportunity for economic advancement, a better life, hope for the future for mankind; peace and justice for all.

I believe the fiftieth state, the bridge between East and West, can help achieve these goals.

ACKNOWLEDGMENTS

The editors desire to express their appreciation to many persons who assisted in the preparation of this book. They risk the hazard in so doing of inadvertently omitting an important name, or names.

They wish to thank:

Dr. Dean C. Allard, Chief Archives Branch, Naval History Division, United States Navy; Malcolm Barr, press secretary to Senator Hiram Fong, of Hawaii; R.E. Bergstrom, a retired Bos'n, of San Diego, who like so many of his shipmates evacuated the *Oklahoma* via porthole; Mrs. Dorothy Bicknell, of Kailua, Hawaii, whose husband, the late Colonel George W. Bicknell, previously assisted in recalling the events immediately before December 7; Mrs. L.V. Bowman, of Ewa, Hawaii, who was listening to a "pastoral" recording at *the* time; Joseph W. Burghard, of Ventura, California, now retired from the Navy, who watched the attack from outside the mobile hospital; Bernard F. Cavalcante, Naval History Division; Miss Agnes Conrad, State Archivist, Honolulu, Hawaii; Mrs. Victoria Custer, Pacific War Memorial Commission, Honolulu; Thomas H. Dowds, now a Pittsburgh, Pennsylvania, police officer, who was at Schofield when "all hell broke loose"; Rear Admiral Ernest M. Eller, USN (ret.), former Director, Naval History, and Captain Kent Loomis, former Assistant Director; Captain Ellis R. Evans, United States Air Force, Commanding, Bellows Air Force Base; Bert M. Fireman, Arizona Historical Foundation, Tempe, Arizona; Mrs. Charles A. Frances, who was "there," on December 7, now of Rockville, Maryland; Captain Ben R. Gittes, Information Officer, Schofield Barracks; Edward J. Greaney, Jr., Deputy Director, Department of Planning and Economic Development, State of Hawaii; Mrs. Rita Halle, Navy Department Library, Washington;

Mrs. Mary D. Hinrichs, Chief Librarian, Hawaii Newspaper Agency; Otto Horky, President, Alamo Chapter, Pearl Harbor Survivors Association, Indianapolis; Captain Charles King, United States Navy (ret.), Arlington, Virginia; Mrs. Kathleen Lloyd, Naval History Division; Commander Joseph W. Marshall, former Public Affairs, Department of Defense; Allan C. McGill, Office of Information, Pacific Fleet; Addis R. McPherson, Homestead Air Force Base, Florida, who drew on his memories of December 7 at Schofield Barracks as a technical adviser to the filming of "From Here to Eternity"; Captain James D. Miller, New Orleans, who was on the *Arizona*; Mrs. E.B. Mitchell, Little Falls Library, Montgomery County, Maryland; Roger S. Moran, of Thorndike, Maine, who was at Hickam Field; William B. Murphy, Chief, Public Information, Hickam Air Force Base; Captain Victor J. Niiranen, Dental Officer, Pacific Fleet; Earl Nishimura, with Senator Fong; Mrs. Thomas J. Nixon, III, of Wilson, North Carolina; Mrs. Frank T. Ostenberg, Alexandria, Virginia; Timothy E. Rowan, Office of Information, Department of the Air Force; Lieutenant Jerry R. Ryan, Public Affairs, Pacific Fleet; George R. Sanner, Jr., President, Maryland Chapter, Pearl Harbor Survivors Association, Bethesda, Maryland; David Schon, Historical Archives, Air Force, Washington; Richard L. Stewart, "late" of the destroyer *Downes,* now oceanographer for the Pacific Fleet; Mrs. Nancy S. Sutterfield, Librarian, Department of Education, State of Hawaii; J. Neil Stoutenburgh. of Washington, who arrived with the 25th Division; Commander Wilmer Thompson, USNR (ret.), then with the public works; Colonel Charles C. Underwood, Information Officer, United States Army, Pacific, who survived Bataan, the death march and a Japanese prison; and Lieutenant Colonel Robert A. Zehring, Chief, Public Information Division, Pacific Air Forces.

Betty Shinn and Karol Zipple, freelance writers of Washington, provided research. editing and typing, assisted by other staffers of the Army Times Publishing Company.

BIBLIOGRAPHY | PRINCIPAL BOOKS CONSULTED

Allen, Gwenfread, *Hawaii's War Years, 1941-1945,* University of Hawaii Press, Honolulu, 1950

Army Times, Editors of, *A History of the United States Signal Corps,* G.P. Putnam's Sons, New York, 1961

Barber, Joseph, *Restless Rampart,* Bobbs-Merrill Company, New York, 1941

Brassey's Naval Annual, London, 1942

Burtness, Paul S. (ed.), *The Puzzle of Pearl Harbor,* Row, Peterson, Evanston, Illinois, 1962

Cant, Gilbert, *America's Navy in World War II,* John Day Company, New York, 1943

Casey, Robert J., *Battle Below,* Bobbs-Merrill Company, New York, 1945

Clark, Blake, *Remember Pearl Harbor!* Harper & Brothers, New York, 1943

Clark, Sydney, *All the Best in Hawaii,* Dodd, Mead & Company, New York, 1961

Cushing, John, *Captain William Matson,* Newcomen Society, Princeton, New Jersey, 1939

Damon, Ethel M., *Sanford Ballard Dole and His Hawaii,* Pacific Books, for Hawaiian Historical Society, Palo Alto, California, 1957

Davids, Jules, *America and the World of Our Time,* Random House, New York, 1960

Day, A. Grove, *Hawaii and Its People,* (revised edition), Meredith Press, New York, 1968

Day, A. Grove and Stroven, Carl (eds.), *Hawaiian Reader,* with introduction by James Michener, Appleton-Century-Crofts, Inc., New York, 1959

Department of Planning and Economic Development, State of Hawaii, *The State of Hawaii Data Book*, Honolulu, 1968

Fane, Commander Francis Douglas, *The Naked Warriors*, Appleton-Century-Crofts Inc., New York, 1956

Farrell, Andrew (ed.), *Memoirs of the Hawaiian Revolution, of Sanford Ballard Dole*, Honolulu Advertiser Publishing Company, Ltd., Honolulu, 1936

Farrow, John, *Damien the Leper*, Sheed & Ward, New York, 1937

Feis, Herbert, *The Road to Pearl Harbor*, Princeton University Press, Princeton, 1950

Forgy, Howell M., *And Pass the Ammunition*, Appleton-Century Co., New York, 1944

Frank, Gerold, *USS Seawolf*, G.P. Putnam's Sons, New York, 1945

Frank, Pat and Harrington, Joseph D., *Rendezvous at Midway*, John Day, New York, 1967

Grew, Joseph C., *Turbulent Era*, Houghton Mifflin, Boston, 1952

Hart, Robert, *The Great White Fleet*, Little, Brown & Company, Boston, 1965

Hashimoto, Mochitsura, *Sunk, the Story of the Japanese Submarine Fleet, (1941-45)*, Henry Holt and Co., New York, 1954

Hodge, Clarence L. (ed.), *Army Life in Hawaii*, Tongg Publishing Company, Honolulu, 1943

Hoehling, A.A., *The Week Before Pearl Harbor*, Norton Company, New York, 1963

Karig, Walter and Kelley, Welbourn, *Battle Report: Pearl Harbor to the Coral Sea*, Farrar & Rinehart, Inc., New York, 1944

Kimmel, Husband E., *Admiral Kimmel's Story*, Regnery Co., Chicago, 1955

Konoye, Fumimaro, *The Memoirs of Prince Fumimaro Konoye*, Okuyama Service, Tokyo, 1945

Langer, William L., *The Undeclared War, 1940-1941*, Harper, New York, 1953

Lee, W. Storrs, *The Islands*, Holt, Rinehart and Winston, New York, 1966

Lee, W. Storrs (ed.), *Hawaii*, Literary Chronicle, Funk & Wagnalls, New York, 1967

Lockwood, Charles H., *Sink 'Em All*, E.P. Dutton, New York, 1951

Lord, Walter, *Day of Infamy*, Holt, Rinehart and Winston, New York, 1957

Lord, Walter, *Incredible Victory*, Harper & Brothers, New York, 1967

MacArthur, Douglas, *Reminiscences*, McGraw-Hill, New York, 1964

Marie, Sister Adele, *To You from Hawaii,* Fort Orange Press, Albany, New York, 1950

Miller, John Jr., Carroll, Owen J. and Tackley, Margaret E., *Korea, 1951-53,* Office of the Chief of Military History, Department of Army, U.S. Government Printing Office, Washington, D.C., 1956

Millis, Walter, *This Is Pearl,* William Morrow & Company, New York, 1947

Michener, James A., *Hawaii,* Secker & Warburg, London, 1960

Morgenstern, George, *The Story of the Secret War,* Devin-Adair, New York, 1947

Morison, Samuel Eliot, *The Two-Ocean War,* Little, Brown & Company, Boston, 1963

Morison, Samuel Eliot, *Coral Sea, Midway and Submarine Actions,* Volume IV of *Naval Operations in World War II,* Little, Brown & Company, Boston, 1959

Pater, Alan F., *United States Battleships,* Monitor Book Company, Beverly Hills, California, 1968

Potter, E.B. and Nimitz, Chester W. (eds.), *The Great Sea War: The Story of Naval Action in World War II,* Prentice-Hall, Englewood Cliffs, New Jersey, 1960

Ridgway, Matthew B., General, United States Army (Ret.), *The Korean War,* Doubleday & Company, Inc., Garden City, New York, 1967

Roosevelt, Eleanor, *This I Remember,* Harper & Brothers, New York, 1949

Sakamaki, Kazuo, *I Attacked Pearl Harbor,* Association Press, New York, 1949

Smith, William Ward, *Midway, Turning Point of the Pacific,* Thomas Y. Crowell, New York, 1966

Stoddard, Charles Warren, *The Lepers of Molokai,* Ave Maria Press, Notre Dame, Indiana, 1886

Truman, Harry S., *Memoirs,* Volume II, Doubleday & Company, Inc., Garden City, New York, 1956

Twain, Mark, *Roughing It,* American Publishing Company, Hartford, Connecticut, 1872

U.S. Congress, 79th Congress, 1st and 2nd Sessions, *Hearings Before the Joint Committee on the Investigation of the Pearl Harbor Attack,* Government Printing Office, 1946, 39 vols.

U.S. Congress 79th Congress, 2nd Session, *Report of the Joint Committee on the Investigation of the Pearl Harbor Attack,* Senate Document No. 244, Government Printing Office, 1946

U.S. Military Academy, *A Military History of World War II,* Vol. 2, West Point, New York: U.S. Military Academy, 1953

U.S. Strategic Bombing Survey (Pacific), *The Campaigns of the Pacific War,* Government Printing Office, 1946

Wainwright, Jonathan M., *General Wainwright's Story,* Doubleday, New York, 1946

Wallin, Vice Admiral Homer N. (Ret.), *Pearl Harbor: Why, How Fleet Salvage and Final Appraisal,* Naval History Division, U.S. Navy, Government Printing Office, 1968

Wilkes, Charles, *Narrative of the United States Exploring Expedition, 1838-42,* Vol. IV, Lea and Blanchard, Philadelphia, 1845

Wise, James E., *Ford Island,* U.S. Naval Institute Proceedings, Volume 90, October, 1964

Wohlstetter, Roberta, *Pearl Harbor: Warning and Decision,* Stanford University Press, Stanford, California, 1962

MAGAZINE ARTICLES

Cope, Harley, "Climb Mount Niitaka," *U.S. Naval Institute Proceedings,* Vol. 72, No. 12, December, 1946

Feis, H., "War Came at Pearl Harbor: Suspicions Considered," *Yale Review,* Vol. 45, No. 3, March, 1956

Fuchida, Mitsuo, "I Led the Air Attack on Pearl Harbor," *U.S. Naval Institute Proceedings,* Vol. 78, No. 9, September, 1952

Fukudome, Shigeru, "Hawaii Operation," *U.S. Naval Institute Proceedings,* Vol. 81, No. 12, December, 1955

Layton, E.T., "Rendezvous in Reverse," *U.S. Naval Institute Proceedings,* Vol. 79, No. 5, May, 1953

Millis, Walter, "Two Hours That Changed History," *New York Times Magazine,* December 2, 1956

Phillips, Cabel, "Ten Years Ago This Friday," *New York Times Magazine,* December 2, 1951

Tai, Sing Loo, "How Happen I Were at Pearl Harbor," *U.S. Naval Institute Proceedings,* Vol. 88, December, 1962

Togo, S., "Why Japan Attacked Pearl Harbor," excerpts from *Cause of Japan, U.S. News & World Report,* Vol. 41, August 31, 1956

Ward, Robert E., "The Inside Story of the Pearl Harbor Plan," *U.S. Naval Institute Proceedings,* Vol. 77, No. 12, December, 1951

Yoshikawa, Takeo, "Top Secret Assignment," *U.S. Naval Institute Proceedings,* Vol. 86, No. 12, December, 1960

NEWSPAPERS and PERIODICALS

The Honolulu Advertiser, issues 1941-53

The Honolulu Star-Bulletin, 1941-53

The Honolulu Star-Bulletin Supplement, *Hawaii at War,* two issues, 1942, 1943

Flying Magazine, August, 1951

Harper's, January, 1943, article by Barry Fox

Marine Engineering & Shipping Review, June, 1943

Maui News, 1941-45

Our Navy, January, 1967, William B. Murphy

Saturday Evening Post, October, 1942, serial of Clarence Dickinson's reminiscences

U.S. Naval Institute Proceedings, Vol. 72, No. 11, Washington, D.C., November, 1946